W9-ADS-278

SAINT BENEDICT JOSEPH LABRE

Saint Benedict Joseph Labre

SAINT BENEDICT JOSEPH LABRE

by

AGNES DE LA GORCE

translated by

ROSEMARY SHEED

Sheed & Ward—1952—New York

Nihil Obstat
John J. Walsh, S.J.
Diocesan Censor

Imprimatur
✠ Richard J. Cushing
Archbishop of Boston

Date: 9 December 1951

The Nihil Obstat and the Imprimatur are ecclesiastical declarations that a publication is free of doctrinal or moral error, not a statement of the positive worth, nor an implication that the contents have the Archbishop's approval or recommendation.

Contents

SAINT BENEDICT JOSEPH LABRE

Chapter One

A Village in Artois

THERE is no more mysterious sweetness than the sweetness of sacrifice, and the dead wood of the cross has done more for men's consolation than all the living forests in the world. Could Francis of Assisi have preached to the birds, or sung of sunlight and flowers, if he had not also received the stigmata of Christ's Passion in the loneliness of a bare mountain-top? There is a strange blessedness about every scene of holocaust: the Aventine heights where Saint Alexis the beggar came to die at the foot of his father's palace steps, the friaries of Assisi, the icy parlours at Avila where Saint Teresa used to converse with other ascetics. The sufferings of the saints were the price they paid for their joy. They are not stuck in their niches; they are ruling the Church; they do not belong exclusively to their own small group of worshippers, but to all who suffer, to all who are for the truth. Time was when those insipidly smiling statues hid from us their wounds and their sufferings. But we have come to realise that without these haloed figures the world would be smothered under its own ashes. "Only in the irremediable is there any peace", wrote Jacques Rivière to Alain Fournier. The saints were the bold players who staked their all on a chessboard where what is won is won forever. What they have won is peace. Their radiance tells us so.

There are any number of pious pictures, but not many portraits of the saints. There is one though in Rome, in the Corsini Gallery. It is of a poor man, of vaguely monastic appearance, a tertiary or oblate of some unidentifiable order, whose habit-like robe has picked up the dust of many roads. His arms are crossed in recollection and in sign of obedience. Round his neck is a rosary, hanging loosely down among the folds of the greenish stuff of his robe. His face is white and wasted; there are none of the ecstatic transports the Spaniards depict in their saints. It simply looks as if daily mortification, as steady as the beating of the surf on the pebbles, has worn all human sorrow off this face, to impress on it the eternal sorrow of Christ. And this sorrow has reached its plenitude: perfect joy. Standing before this mysterious portrait one cannot help murmuring, *Consummatum est*. Here is a man who has lived everything to the full, who has known the absolute—in happiness, in suffering, in silence. There is no colour of life in those sunken, terribly emaciated cheeks. But there is a peace that we can scarcely understand. This poor man with nothing to call his own seems to have got all that he wants, and we long to know the secret of his joy. The serenity of his mouth is echoed in the smiling eyes, lowered so that we do not meet their gaze. And yet there is a controlled fire there which gives life to the whole face, as the consecrated bread, hidden in the tabernacle, gives life to a whole Church. We are

A Village in Artois

certain that those eyes we cannot see are bright. We see hair that is bright gold—almost red—in the scraggy beard, the eyebrows and on the head. This ragged solitary whom the painter Antonio Cavallucci met in the streets in Rome was a foreigner in Italy, and clearly a northerner—not the rubicund Flemish type, but another, with a face strangely bony and mortified. This man, lost in prayer, bears the marks of his race. The picture in the Corsini Gallery represents Benedict Joseph Labre, a man from Artois. The name has been made ridiculous, synonymous with verminousness, ignorance and animalism. But this portrait really lays bare the soul, and would in itself be a magnificent justification of a much misunderstood saint—if the saints can be said to have any need to be justified to us.

The plain of Artois, bounded on the north by the mountains of Flanders, was more wooded in the eighteenth century than it is today, and more alive with the ringing of bells—the bells of abbeys and priories no longer there. It is a misty and fertile stretch of land. On fine days there is a pale light, curiously soft and diffused, which can give the momentary illusion that animals and natural objects are somehow detached from the ground.

Among the first foothills of Artois, about five leagues from Béthune, lies a little valley hollowed out by the Nave, a very small tributary of the Lys, with bridges made of logs running across it from the doorways of the houses. The village of Amettes nestles there. Fields marked off by thick hedges, houses tucked away out of sight, an ever-growing store of traditions, ideas not soon

5

changed: everything about the place conspires towards a forcing of the soul in upon itself. And of this village, where everything tends to conserve and to restrict, a contemplative was born.

On March 27, 1748, in this village of Amettes, which belonged of old to the diocese of Boulogne, a newborn—a firstborn—child, was baptised with the names Benedict Joseph.[1] His father, Jean Baptiste Labre, was a comfortably-off farmer—he had some forty acres of land—married to Anne Barbe Gransire, from Artois like himself. Rural communities were assessed by families and by homesteads. In Amettes, the Labre family was the oldest.

Nowadays, in the village of Amettes, one sloping field is set apart as a place of pilgrimage. The porch, the cowsheds, the barns that once surrounded the house where Benedict Joseph Labre was born, are now no more; but the house itself still stands on its steep slope of ground. Germain Nouveau, the poet, described it to his friend Paul Verlaine, remarking how much he wished the old thatched roof had been kept. The house is now open to anyone passing that way—it is simply a sanctuary, alive

---

[1] *L'an 1748, le 27 mars, le soussigné François-Joseph Labre, prêtre, vicaire d'Ames, a baptisé un fils, né le jour précédant en légitime mariage de Jean-Baptiste Labre, marchand mercier et d'Anne-Barbe Grandsir, ses père et mère de cette paroisse, auquel on a imposé le nom de Benoît-Joseph.*

Le parrain a été le dit François-Joseph Labre, baptisant du consentiment du sieur Réant, curé d'Amettes et la marraine Anne-Théodore Hazembergue, femme de Jacques-François Vincent, laboureur, demeurant en cette paroisse, lesquels interrogés s'ils savaient écrire de ce interpellés, ont répondu le savoir. (From the Amettes parish Register for 1748.)

Benedict Joseph Labre's mother signed her name to a letter, the original of which is now in Rome, as *Gransire*. I have therefore chosen this rather than various other spellings.

A Village in Artois

only with holiness. But with a little imagination one can see it as it used to be, full of its family and its affairs.

First the main room: this used to be a shop. Anne Barbe Gransire, Benedict Labre's mother, kept one of those village stores where bales of serge and linen, bonnets and ribbons, lie side by side with sugared almonds in a tiny, oddly assorted display. This was the room where they had their meals and spent their evenings, and one can still hear the walls resounding with their archaic-sounding patois. In a language in which word after word seems to have escaped from Froissart or Commines, the old men would live over again the horrors of the war at the end of Louis XIV's reign. The enemy, commanded by Prince Eugène and the Duke of Marlborough, had captured Béthune, and then laid siege to Aire-sur-la-Lys. Amettes suffered much. The then curé—Monsieur Blondel—has left us an account of what they went through in the village archives:[1]

All the people were so terrified that they left their homes, and all withdrew towards Saint Omer, taking with them their cattle—that is, as much of their cattle as had not been driven off. But we suffered so much during this exile, with the cattle dying of hunger, that, since the looting by the soldiers had stopped, we all decided to go back to our village with the safe-conduct the army gave us, preferring to die in our birthplace or lose all our possessions there, rather than wither away any longer in a strange place where no one would help us. We therefore left Saint Omer on September 7th, and the following day, the dawn found us back at Amettes. When daylight came to give us sight of our village everyone in the

[1] See two articles, "Amettes, patrie d'un saint", in the review *L'Université Catholique* (Feb. 15 and Apr. 15, 1894).

parish was there, and many from other places near by; it would be impossible to convey on paper the joy we felt at the sight of our beloved village. I doubt whether even the Jews' joy could have been greater when they saw Jerusalem again after their long and hard captivity. But our joy was shortlived.

Yet another affliction came upon the starving community: the plague. The Curé Blondel lost most of his parishioners: "Those who come after will never realise the full extent of our misery . . . I can give no exact accounting of the ages of those who died, for there was no time to find out—often the father buried his son, the son his mother, the husband his wife, the wife her daughter—such was the utter confusion of it".

The annals of every province are made up of numberless fresh beginnings: with great difficulty the village was re-created; it never regained its former stature, for now there were only thirty or forty families. And Benedict Labre must have listened through many an evening to this tale of war and plague. But more often there were the old *fabliaux,* there were jokes and songs. The women came with their distaffs; they had nuts and apples to munch; and the rafters gradually grew black from the thick smoke, for the peasants in those parts grew a great deal of tobacco and used it generously. They would be filling their pipes while humming some Christmas carol now forgotten by all but the learned and the very old, or perhaps a lament like *The Wandering Jew.* These simple people had learned the long verses by heart from the brightly coloured sheets of paper the pedlars brought round. The monotonous cadences were soothing, and to men as deeply rooted in their homes as these the sense

A Village in Artois

of an everlasting journey about the world brought on a
strange musing:

> *Est-il rien sur la terre*
> *Qui soit plus surprenant*
> *Que la grande misère*
> *Du pauvre Juif Errant? . . .*

A primitive lamp—an iron shell full of oil with a
lighted wick soaking in it—shone on the same objects
you would find on the mantelpiece of any peasant's home:
a crucifix, some holy pictures, painted plates, pewter pots.
In the half-light one could just glimpse the bin which
held the bread made in the bakehouse close by.

In Artois, the right of primogeniture held good for
peasant as for gentleman. Benedict, as the eldest, was
heir to the house, the stables, the fields, and the chests
and strong-boxes. This was not heaven marking out a
chosen one; it was earth handing on the privileges of
head of one small family. There was no hint of supernatural predestination. However, Benedict had an uncle,
Jacques Joseph Vincent, who was alight with that mystical fire which can eclipse the faithful vigil-light of tradition and eat up the whole of a man's life. This young
man wanted to be a Franciscan, but his father set all
his paternal authority against the idea. Jacques Vincent
was shattered, but dutifully, and in the name of obedience,
he agreed to become a secular priest instead. The small
boy Benedict often went to see his grandmother[1] who
lived in a farm called La Cauchiette, right at the end

[1] Anne Hazembergues, widow of Denis Gransire, Benedict Labre's
maternal grandmother, who had married for the second time a farmer
called Vincent.

of the village beside what used to be the Brunehaut road. And it was there that Jacques Joseph Vincent was living, until he should be old enough to be ordained. It was he who first taught Benedict how to pray, and with disturbing seriousness imparted to him his sense of God's greatness.

There is an expression still in use among the peasants of Artois which must surely have been familiar to Benedict: *Il faut aller servir. Aller servir* meant to set out upon a pilgrimage. As a child Benedict assimilated quite naturally the religious traditions around him. Was the earth niggardly with her harvests? *Il faut aller servir Notre Dame Panetière,* he heard the farmers saying. In the town of Aire, with its *béguinages* along the banks of the Lys, Notre Dame Panetière had fed her people through the famines of old. If someone was suffering from fever or from eczema, one "went to wait upon" Saint Isberga, King Charlemagne's sister, who was as lovely as a fairy-tale princess, and to whom God granted leprosy to disfigure her, so that the world would no longer find her pleasing. And Benedict also knew the story of Saint Bertha, who was invoked from afar for any disease of the eyes. In Merovingian times this royal widow had founded the monastery of Blangy-sur-Ter-noise which, in the eighteenth century, belonged to the Benedictines. Two of her daughters became nuns. The third, Saint Emma, married an English prince who treated her abominably and reduced her to the state of a slave. Repudiated once and for all, she tried to come back to her mother, but died on the way. The boat bearing her body sailed up the river Canche, and Saint Bertha and her nuns came with great pomp to meet it. "Alas, daughter", said the abbess, as she saw the stiff body being carried towards her on the waves, "my eyes see you, but yours will never see again!" Whereat, the legend says, the closed eyelids of the dead woman flickered open for a second.

If he heard these stories, Benedict Labre certainly believed every word. Such medieval legends cannot really have meant a great deal to him—any influences he underwent were close at hand and far less poetic—but they inspired in him the most perfect obedience to God's commands. To this child of eighteenth-century Artois, a miracle was the flowering of hope, and a breath of pride would wither it. And when such a flower sprung from his own hands it never shook his humility for a moment.

The church of Amettes itself was the scene of an obscure pilgrimage to St. Catherine of Alexandria; it contained relics that had been brought from the East. Its Gothic tower stands out proudly against the hill where the graveyard lies. The nave today is just as it was then: you can see the font where Benedict was brought for baptism, the confessional where he knelt, the pulpit he turned to face. The altar where he served Mass was decorated with a very indifferent picture whose meaning would be far clearer to Benedict than to most of us: it depicted a priest raising the host, with two altar-boys holding the hem of his chasuble. From the side of a crucified Christ a stream of blood poured out to refresh and to save souls in the fire of Purgatory. And Benedict meditated on the mystery of that blood, on the mystery of that fire. He saw these suffering souls close to the altar, just as they were in that not very impressive painting. The august movements at which he assisted, the ritual words to which he gave the responses, extended across eternity, from the heights to the depths. And when the other boys, who had no such intuitive realisation, prevented him from serving Mass to tease him and to cross him because his fervour so far outran their own, he suffered intensely: though so young, he felt love's jealousy. In the church of Amettes he prayed like a child in the arms of unseen powers. He was given the gift of perfect joy. But he did not realise it, and the joy had to be taken from him before he discovered how sweet it was.

Because his family was so important in the village, because he was an eldest son, and because he was so honest and so thoughtful, Benedict held a position of preeminence among the other children, and was to some extent their model. As a reward for good behaviour, Anne Barbe Gransire would sometimes take him with her to the market at Lillers, and he would hear her haggling over prices like the thrifty peasant she was. And Benedict advised her to do it in some other way—"in case", he said, "the dealer might be paid less than was due him, or might feel called upon to lie".[1] He criticised most severely the smallest deceit or dishonesty. Choosing examples from his mother's shop-counter, he used to say to his fellow schoolboys: "You begin by taking thread, then needles, then scissors and finally money". And with terrifying logic, he would add: "And in the end you go to hell".

From the accounts we have of his childhood, Benedict Labre seems to have been of a fiery disposition, and a scrupulous austerity which became more and more

[1] From Anne Barbe Gransire's statement at the preliminary process in Boulogne, 1784.

marked up to the crisis of adolescence. His mother noted that he purposely sat far from the fire on the most bitterly cold evenings; and when the local holiday—the *ducasse*—came round, and the tarts, as tradition prescribed, were making in the bakehouse, his will to penance asserted itself more strongly still. And yet he liked—and quite intensely I think—the fire burning in the hearth of the damp cottage and the appetising pastry his mother made. But from the first awakening of his mind, his young uncle, the would-be Franciscan, had impressed on him the idea of mortification.

The people he lived among were honest, but unpolished, quick to quarrel when the beer flowed; there were feasts which turned into brawls, there were urchins who used to take their stations along a trench to throw stones at their eternal enemies, the urchins of the next village.

When Benedict was twelve, his family decided what his future was to be. His parents took great pride in this child, so much cleverer and better-behaved than the others. In him the characteristics of his race were at their best. In the province of Artois, every parish had a school which was directly supervised by the priests. The master was a cleric, assisted by some layman chosen by the assembly of villagers—the *lay-cleric,* who chanted at the lectern and tolled the bells. The curate of Amettes, François d'Hanutel, and his assistant, a certain Forgeois, taught Benedict the rudiments. He had an alphabet-book with two utterly naïve pictures on the cover, of heaven and hell; he soon learnt to read, write and count. The school was a mixed one, with the boys sitting on one side, the girls on the other. Benedict betook himself to the shabby premises with an eagerness to learn which struck everyone who knew him as a child. He was not merely an intelligent pupil, said his masters, but the most intelligent they had ever come across. He used to set off in the winter fog, with an armful of wood—for all the scholars had to give something towards heating the school. Their books were mainly of religious instruction: a catechism, a Life of Christ, an abridged version of the Old Testament, or perhaps the *Flowers of the Saints,* by the Spanish Jesuit Ribadeneira—which edifying work was handed down from generation to generation. Sometimes, to help the children to read every sort of script, the masters would let them examine one of the church psalters, or some document from the village archives: a contract set down on paper or parchment, or perhaps a title-deed. The classes were always brought to an end with the Salve Regina.

Benedict worked so hard, and the curate spoke so highly of his intelligence, that his parents decided to send him to school at Nédon, the next village, because the school there did not close during harvest-time, as did the one at Amettes. Was Benedict to be a farmer like his father? That would seem to be the natural thing: he was the eldest, the natural successor. However, the old order was coming to an end, and the peasant tending to become detached from his land. A less religious father than Jean Baptiste Labre might well have wanted his son to become a priest as a means of rising socially. The Labre parents were quite ready to see this devout child of theirs, so curiously avid for learning, as a future parish priest of a village—that is, as a zealous servant of God, but also perhaps as a man of influence and high esteem who would provide for the education of his brothers and sisters—of whom there were already a large number. And there were to be yet more, for Anne Barbe Gransire was to give birth to fifteen children in all.

Life became less comfortable in the Amettes household. One day Jean Baptiste Labre fell ill, and his brother, a priest, came to see him. He was Benedict's godfather, had formerly been a curate at Ames, and was now parish priest of Erin. He too thought he could see in his godson the marks of a vocation to the priesthood, and he offered his parents to take him home with him and take on the expenses of bringing him up. A year of bad luck for a family with material cares pressing heavily upon them, a generous uncle coming to call and assuming the charge of a child—it was the beginning of a spiritual adventure whose end was to be the canonisation of a saint.

Benedict followed his uncle to the village of Erin, near Saint-Pol. And in the six years that followed, he was to return home only at rare intervals, not always even for every *ducasse*—the festival when all the villagers gathered where their fathers lay buried and ended a day of uproar with the De Profundis.

Chapter Two

The Library of a Priest's House

A SMALL bell rings, a man and a child walk across the rich Artois fields—Father François Labre and his godson are taking Holy Communion to someone sick.

It was quite usual for a priest to have living with him some child who hoped vaguely, or perhaps quite definitely, to become a priest. There would sometimes be two or three together. And the villagers had a good deal of respect for these small boys who were not going to till the earth, and who walked through the fields carrying their Latin grammars. Benedict Labre was a perfect example of this sort of schoolboy emerged from the status of peasant into the rural bourgeoisie which bore the priest at its summit.

Benedict began to learn what were the various things expected of a country priest. He had to give his parishioners moral advice, but also from time to time judicial and even medicinal help: he kept a medicine chest, and knew something of curative herbs. His knowledge often helped towards agricultural developments. It was his work to keep the civil state Registers. He could receive

16

wills. In cases of famine or plague, or when there was an epidemic among the cattle, he had to inform the authorities and ask for help. For the villagers he was their link not only with the Mystical Body, but also with the centre of the nation. The Sunday sermon was more than likely to turn into a civic instruction: the priest became a newspaper for the illiterate. "The king's troops . . . . the king's illness . . . . the king's recovery . . . ." The peasants heard the word repeated with great respect; they had faith in the anointing of Rheims. When the queen gave birth to a son their voices joyfully took up the Te Deum intoned by the priest; and when, as in 1765, after the dauphin's death, those same voices were raised in the psalm of mourning, they shivered at the thought that God's anger might be descending upon the dynasty that embodied France. Little Benedict had heard the hymn of triumph sung for the newborn princes, for the Duc de Berry, the Comte d'Artois, and the Comte de Provence. It must have seemed as if only the trumpets of Judgment Day could interrupt this alternation of Te Deum and De Profundis.

All too often the priest's temporal duties swamped his spiritual work and reduced it to almost nothing. The parish priest of the *Dictionnaire philosophique* was scarcely more than an enlightened philanthropist—and an apothecary for good measure—who would join in a game of bowls or tennis on Sundays on the lawn in front of the church. He never gave a thought to dogma, and got through all the ceremonies as fast as he could. What he believed hardly mattered, for the existence of God was necessary "for princes and for their peoples" and confession was "a curb on crime"! He was celibate out of respect for longstanding custom. A certain amount of hypocrisy became him. When he went to see a play at the neighbouring château "he sat behind a grille so as not to give scandal to the weaker brethren".

Abbé François Labre had nothing in common with this indulgent and worldly minister of religion. He cared tremendously about dogma; he hoped that unbelief would be conquered by knowledge. Unbelief! Benedict heard the word and said it over to himself without understanding it. The only mists he knew were those that lay on the fields. His godfather gave him a solid basis of knowledge; he was a doctor of theology, and, what mattered more, a very holy priest. Benedict used to go through the village with his uncle to the bedsides of the sick, while children ran after to kiss the hands that touched the Host. He helped him in everything he did. At weddings and baptisms he was often asked to sign his name as a witness in the parish registers. Quite unwittingly, by his youth and his gentle thoughtfulness, he gained for himself a popularity which was destined to carry on that of his uncle. For would he not later take his place in that same parish? So everyone thought. The Princess de Croÿ, who lived in the château in the woods outside the village, used, with a protective gesture, to call him her Little Curé.

One day a great noise of riders and drums heralded, as was customary, a visitation from the bishop. The Bishop of Boulogne at that time was Mgr. de Partz de Pressy. He was a man much praised for his kindness— only a short while before he had tried to protect from the law some poor wretch who had tried to assassinate him. Bishop de Partz de Pressy confirmed Benedict Labre, who had just made his first Communion. The Curé of Erin must certainly have pointed out to the bishop with great pride this nephew he was preparing for the priesthood, this student for whom there was nothing but praise. The bishop gave his blessing.

And, without doubt, Benedict Labre would have made an exemplary parish priest in Artois, had it not been for the tempest that was to burst upon his soul. The upheaval that took place when he was fourteen was set in two scenes, two solitudes, the presbytery garden and its library. It was a wonderful garden for fruit. But, while picking up windfalls he was seized by a scruple, a child's scruple, to be sure, but of crucial importance nonetheless, for he saw in these fruits a symbol of all the sense-delights offered to man. It was not surprising that all his pane-gyrists made so much of the ripe cherries and apricots he denied himself. The violence he used upon himself tells us how passionate was his nature and how very much he would have enjoyed those fruits. Benedict Labre was never a schoolboy on holiday, feeling through the dew for hidden strawberries. He was always curbing himself, al-ways holding back, not out of indifference, but because his vocation already demanded that he give up all pleasures —a vocation which came to change the destiny of a peasant linked to the soil. So with Joan of Arc, so with Bernadette. Here was nothing dazzling, no waving of banners, no smile from Our Lady; only the gaping wounds of Christ for Benedict to shelter in. One almost feels that the young man was surrounded by a circle of shadow where grass and flowers could only wither. All Benedict was in future to see was a landscape of ashes and the cross of our

Redemption. The only way to express this laying waste of everything before him is to quote Saint Paul's words: "I make up in my flesh what is wanting to the sufferings of Christ".

What we try to analyse, what we endeavour to take apart each with our own prism, Benedict *felt* quite supernaturally, very simply. He allowed himself to be influenced by what he read: books will not tranform us unless we are prepared to let them. It was only because Benedict Labre was already a penitent, already had an obscure realisation that his vocation was to expiate, that he could be overwhelmed by a collection of sermons.

The library of the Erin presbytery was full of hundred-year-old books, the great spiritual writings of the seventeenth century. It was a favourite spot with Benedict, who contrived to be alone as much as possible, not because he was unsociable, but because his life was becoming more and more an inward and ever-deepening colloquy with God. It had begun by being a sort of holy fear. Beside him in that library there rose the voice of a preacher who had been a century dead, Père Le Jeune. Père Le Jeune was further removed from Labre's day than, say, Chateaubriand is from ours. The whole tempo was different; customs, fashions, books, but Benedict had no wish to differentiate between the old and the modern.

Père Le Jeune was born in 1592, the son of a member of the Judiciary Council of Dôle. He was one of the first members of the Oratory, founded in France by Cardinal de Bérulle. To us he seems a harsh saint for a harsh age. While he was still a young priest, giving the Lenten sermons in Rouen Cathedral, a blackness descended upon him which was to remain: he became blind. Henceforward he was nicknamed Père l'Aveugle—the Blind Father —and that was the name by which Benedict knew him. He was still allowed to say Mass, but he did not wish to. "For fear of committing some irreverence", wrote his disciple, Père Reuben, "he died of thirst beside the living spring". However, he continued preaching. He travelled all over France, but his apostolate was most active in the central provinces. He died at Limoges in his eighties, and the populace proclaimed this ascetic a saint. His mortifications revolt us. When Benedict read the panegyric which was included in the volume of sermons, he must have understood the towering horror of the lines: "We saw him, still as a statue, submitting to be devoured by the vermin which are the inseparable accompaniment of poverty and penitential old age".[1] One day, highwaymen broke into Père Le Jeune's coach and wounded him; on another occasion while crossing a river, his litter was swept into the water. Whether bleeding, soaked to the skin, shaking with fever, or bent double with rheumatism, and blind though he was, he always went at once to the church to proclaim to his hearers that only the soul mattered, that the rest of man was nothing: "Is there anything in the world of greater value than a human soul? . . . What *could* be worth more than you, and all other men, saving only Him who made you and all creation?" If man presumes to revolt against this necessary arrangement of things, then chaos sets in. From the well-ordered society of his day the preacher borrowed examples to describe a world turned upside down: "Supposing, in this Republic, imbeciles were put in place of judges, supposing aristocrats and men

---

[1]Père Reuben, *Discours funèbre sur la vie et la mort du P. Le Jeune* (1684).

of letters were forced to plough the earth, what confusion and difficulty would not result?"

Penance could reestablish order even after the most frightful discord had disturbed it. Père Le Jeune was a master at touching the chord of heroism in a man's soul. His century was not one of discretion, of shades of meaning, or of conciliation. In the theatres of the day, lit by the flickering of candles, Don Diego was preaching honour, Horace was preaching patriotism, and the martyr Polyeuctus was preaching fidelity even unto death. It is hardly surprising that Père Le Jeune preached penance with an absoluteness worthy of Corneille. "Suffering rides pillion with sin", he used to say. He urged expiation upon everyone, and it seemed that as far as he was concerned, it knew no limits. He allowed no pity for the maltreated body. In fact, he conceded man the right to shorten his life by mortification: "If the flesh wars against the spirit and offers it baits which may lose it eternal life, why should not the soul fight against it, and perhaps even shorten its temporal life?" This grim principle was to be law as far as Benedict Labre was concerned. This Oratorian missionary, whether speaking to country gentry, to Auvergne or Limousin farmers, threw them for food the story of Saint Jerome bruising his own chest with a stone. The gate of heaven became horribly narrow. Who could get through it? The martyr eaten by lions, Saint Simeon Stylites, at last come down from his pillar. But what of the rest? Sinners must quake. Père Le Jeune proposed to his hearers the most weighty examinations of conscience: "When you kill the father of a family, when you take away a widow's belongings . . ." But the just were not to feel content, either: let them examine the

The Library of a Priest's House

good deeds they were so proud of and make sure there was no evil lurking behind them, that they were not in reality leading towards damnation. And, in all sincerity, he beat his own breast, too. He preached fear, and the same fear seized himself. This man, blind and ill, looking towards the last, Père Reuben tells us "like a worm coiling itself up to die", had his hearers close to tears as he cried:

I imagine when I preach to you that I am doing it for God, but perhaps I am not seeking Him at all: I imagine that I am not seeking worldly glory, but perhaps that is what I am going after all the time. O God, give me grace not to seek it! I try often to commend to Christ the backmost recesses of my soul, for it is a labyrinth, an abyss, a bottomless pit.

The psychological pessimism characteristic of the French—particularly those writers in the seventeenth century who studied the human heart with such minuteness—tends to put the doctrine of original sin in a place of gloomy primacy. There was a constant delving into that inmost recess, that labyrinth, that abyss where all was corruption. Père Le Jeune had many personal ties with Port Royal. His enemies called him a Jansenist, and he suffered deeply over this unjust accusation. That he was a rigourist was due to the country and the century he was born in. He did not always, in his sermons, keep a perfect balance between hope and fear, between blessing and anathematizing, between the joy of redemption and fear of punishment. The infant Saviour in the crib was too often eclipsed by the Judge launching his thunderbolts. And yet in the natural style of Père l'Aveugle there was a kind of amiable scolding, which, though rough, yet had enough humour in it to dispel fear; it was the matter-of-factness of an age still young, still close to the people. When the missionary wanted to describe how souls which reject grace may eventually be abandoned, he illustrates this tragic reality by an informal and almost amusing picture of home life: "If your servant were to say to you: Sir, for two years I have, as you told me to, been taking your son a candle every morning in the winter at five, so that he can get up and study; but I can tell you that he does nothing of the sort; he leaves it burning on the table and sleeps on till seven. If, as I say, your servant said this, you would tell him not to take the candle any more". But this preacher of punishments was also something of a poet. He decried human things for their delusion and emptiness. He showed how the immense sacrifices he asked were tiny things, lost in the passing of time. His words here take on the movement of a rising tide:

When men sail down the Garonne, or the Loire, or the Seine, as long as they remain on the river it seems to them extremely wide, but when they have passed the river mouth and sailed out into the sea, and look at the wide, the vast expanse of the ocean before them the river seems very narrow indeed. Thirty or forty years ago, when you were young, you often became absorbed in things which seemed of immense importance then, but which you can see now were the merest trifles. You were hotheaded, you were enraged over some dispute for heaven knows what, over a question of precedence, or some tiny point of honour, and now looking back upon it it seems only a dream; and when you have spent five hundred, fifteen hundred, ten thousand years, in eternity and look back upon this life and all you did during it, it too will seem to have been a dream.

The Library of a Priest's House

Père Le Jeune always remained a humanist: here and there in his sermons he would draw some moral from the classics that would have surprised the ancients. He loved nature very much as St. Francis of Sales did. In the same tones, with the same charm, he sang the praises of that humility which wins heaven:

There are some birds with magnificent wings, which could fly very high to build their nests on top of rocks, or in trees, and who yet build them in the earth, or in bushes, among thorns and exposed to every sort of danger, whereas the lizard, which has no wings, scales walls with only its legs to support it, and often makes its home in the houses of the great, in mansions and palaces.

As he read these lines, in the library of the presbytery, surely Benedict Labre must have lost all his fears, his longing to hide, to make himself nothing. But in Artois he had never seen a lizard slipping from rock to rock under a blazing sun. The occasional mildness of Père l'Aveugle struck home far less than his threats. The preacher gave to every text of scripture its strictest possible meaning: "Yes, indeed", he went so far as to say, "many will be damned; few will be saved". These words were flung out in the church of some village, perhaps difficult of access, to a congregation where scruples were almost unknown—escaped criminals might even be taking refuge there. Now, a century later, the same words struck deep into the soul of Benedict Labre, innocent of the innocent. From the time of his meditating on these sermons we always see the village schoolboy linked with the ghost of Père Le Jeune. He was a young man preparing for the priesthood who practised mortification, but this book turned him into a full-time penitent. All his thoughts were now turned towards the cloister, though which cloister he was not as yet clear; and yet he tried to put the idea from him, for he knew it clashed with what his parents wanted. It was the first, the negative vocation of fear. Benedict sought shelter from sin as one looks for cover during a storm. To keep alive what he considered a salutary fear, he learnt by heart those sermons which dealt with hell and spoke of how few souls were to be saved. For all that Père Le Jeune had to say about an eternity of unhappiness, Benedict could find analogies in the penal laws of the day: the shame of the pillory, the agony of the wheel or the red-hot pincers, the stinking horror of the dungeons, "the swearing and the din among the galley convicts". What Benedict derived from all this was no merely physical terror. He feared no torture more than he feared being cut off from God, the only Good. He was never without one of these volumes in his hand, and they were to him a long manual of fear, but also a breviary of adoration. Père Le Jeune was a disciple of Cardinal de Bérulle and once he had sufficiently terrorised his hearers would lead them on to the mystical doctrine inherited from him. In Benedict, this doctrine came as a seed which was to bear fruit only much later. For the moment its only work was to add desire of heaven to his simple fear of hell.

In the Erin presbytery, Benedict one day sat reading. No scene could have been more peaceful. Such murmurings as broke the silence seemed only part of it. All of a sudden discord broke out. Benedict lifted his head; he had heard those shouts before. Father François Labre

The Library of a Priest's House

was away that day; his servant was abusing the beggars: "Tramps . . . Lazy good-for-nothings. . . ." Each rebuke was followed by a confused noise of supplication. Benedict leant out of the window and saw the troop of beggars, a familiar sight. They were a public nuisance—and well he knew it—these wretched bands who came to the abbeys and pestered the monks till they fed them. In 1768 the Superior Council of Artois made a terrifying decree—one of those decrees meant more as a bogey than anything else—against anyone homeless and out of work found begging. When he had been imprisoned once he could be branded with a red-hot iron with a letter that showed his degradation, and the third time he was caught, he could be sent to the galleys. But a Christ cannot look upon beggars as would an economist or a legislator. Bishop de Partz de Pressy, at the very time when these harsh laws were being set up, spoke in his pastoral letter of "the extraordinary number of poor people". He excused all the disturbances they made on the ground that these were "the result of avarice". In heart-breaking terms he pleaded their cause: "Their humble supplications, their mournful tones, their groaning and their sighs, show us all too clearly that they need our help to keep them alive".

"Tramps! Robbers!", shouted the priest's servant, "scoundrels!" Benedict had heard of farmyards being pillaged, of barns and hayricks fired. The peasants made arrangements to take it in turns to stand guard over their goods. They took down the guns hanging over their mantelpieces. And yet, in the book Benedict had just laid down, Père Le Jeune preached heroic almsgiving, just as he preached penance, the kind of almsgiving

Pascal and Saint Vincent de Paul had in mind: "The chosen soul, when he finds a poor man in the street, filthy, lacerated, wan, stinking and covered in vermin, brings him into his house, sets him near his fire, washes him and puts him to rights; a worldly soul would find this astounding. Whence is the difference? The chosen soul knows the hidden meaning of poverty". *The hidden meaning of poverty*—its eminent dignity in the Church, as Bossuet called it—was essentially redemptive, and that was what fortified Benedict. A moment earlier he had heard ringing through his head like warning bells the often repeated words *gehenna, souls in sin, everlasting death*. And now these beggars were going by. "Give, give to our Queen . . .": the tune was the tune of a popular lament, the voices those of beggars of Artois mixed in with tramps who called no country their own; they asked for nothing in their own name. To go near these vagrants Benedict had to get over an instinctive repugnance. Their vermin nauseated him, for he was naturally fastidious. But he saw this act of charity as a pledge of heaven. In these poor down-and-outs, whom he knew he had no right to judge, he saw Christ's suffering messengers: he was ready to kiss their sores.

"Are you so poor", queried Père Le Jeune's voice out of the past, "are you so poor that you can give *nothing?*"

Benedict was only a student; he had no savings and lived dependent upon the generosity of his family. He could at least call these wretches and give them what he had in his purse, his bread and the food prepared for his next meal. The servant stopped cursing the beggars, and under his breath turned his fury on this young man whose goodness shamed him, and whom he hated far more than any of them. They for their part moved off, blessing the priest's nephew. Among the tramps was one who looked quite different from the others. He stood apart, telling his beads, and promising prayers in return for any food given him. Was he returning from Blangy-sur-Ternoise, from the shrine of Saint Bertha? Or was he on his way to the village of Allouagne to venerate the Holy Tear which Christ wept over Lazarus? Perhaps he was no better than the others; perhaps he, too, if given a chance, would steal a rabbit or a duck from a farm where he found shelter. He was a pilgrim.

The change in Benedict had been wholly interior. As far as the peasants could see he was the same placid northerner he always had been; he had entered upon a path not of pessimism, but of expiation. He was particularly skilled to find the right words when people needed comforting, and for this he gradually developed more and more sweetness and power. The more he feared for his own last end, the more he cheered and reassured others in their earthly worries, their ordinary human miseries. One small girl, with the typical Artois name of Austreberthe Delplanque, was in floods of tears because her stepmother would not let her go to school. Benedict urged her to be submissive. Together they knelt in the church and prayed, and from that day forward the child accepted her disappointment without a murmur. Benedict fully sympathised with her. How much would he have suffered a while ago had he been forbidden to go to school! Indeed, how now explain his sudden aversion to studying Latin? The cadences of Cicero and the poetry of Virgil, like the fruit in the garden, seemed something he must deny himself. He suddenly found himself feeling miserable during his uncle's learned instructions, at the thought that he was taking time from his deepest love, from the passion whose flame was not of this earth, but shone with the white brightness of the stars. Father François Labre did not as yet reproach his godson for this. He had never before shown any signs of laziness, and this might merely have been the natural lassitude of adolescence—he was, after all, still growing.

Before he reached the stated age Benedict kept the fasting laws of the Church; he allowed himself no amusements. His uncle was somewhat disturbed by this excessive leaning towards austerity, but never for a moment feared it as Jansenistic. To him Jansenism was a living and ever-present reality. He had several times given his adherence to the bull *Unigenitus* by one of those oaths of orthodoxy occasionally demanded of the clergy, worded to fit the particular heresy being attacked at a given time. In this particular diocese there had been the bitterest theological disputes. A certain ascetic and over-scrupulous Bishop of Boulogne, Pierre de Langle, was noted for his zeal for the Jansenist cause and steady opposition to the bull *Unigenitus;* he had died forty years earlier, but left disciples whom the High Court protected. The present Bishop, Mgr. de Partz de Pressy, strongly condemned them. There were, then, priests scattered around the countryside who incurred the censure of their bishop, dissenters unknown to us whose names may have been familiar to Benedict. He must, if so, have condemned them with the uncompromisingness of his youth, for his whole family were deeply attached to Bishop de Partz de Pressy. There was an immense gulf between the spiritual

The Library of a Priest's House

school that Port Royal was at the beginning and the party with its many factions which now stood for Jansenism. How could Benedict and his uncle see the smallest connection between their insubordinate contemporaries and that saint of the past, Père l'Aveugle? And yet the respect for the sacraments that the old missionary father taught was dangerously like the fear that paralyses: "When you hear Mass, when you go to Communion, tremble, for you are working out your salvation. . . . Be careful that you perform these actions well, be careful lest you confess, or communicate, unworthily".

Those destined to become saints do not breathe the pure air of the angels, but the same dusty stuff as the rest of us. The country Benedict Labre came from was a country where words did not come easily, where the silences were heavy, the laughter loud, where the people were faithful but seldom joyful. It was a climate for scruples just as it was a climate for mists. This child of Artois entered upon a great trial: the torment of knowing himself unworthy of Holy Communion. Until the day when God's peace triumphed in his soul he was to drag this torment with him from church to church.

At Erin, Abbé François Labre, despite his reputation of being strict in the confessional and giving harsh penances[1], set his nephew's mind at rest, and sent him to the Communion rail. With the same movement of generosity and pity for the fears of youth, he made him promise to enjoy himself on days of village holiday-making. And Benedict came with this intention into the

[1] Extract from a letter from the Second List of the miracles worked through the intercession of the Venerable Benedict Joseph Labre and other fragments, letters and anecdotes (1784).

village square; he would very much have liked to have fun with the rest; but his love was so intense that he could not. Everyone else was making merry, but he could only think of Christ and His loneliness. The dark horror of the world's sins burst upon this innocent child, this Levite brought up in the very shadow of the temple. He did not consider the difference between one sin and another—he scarcely even knew what they were called. He left his companions. Kneeling at the foot of a crucifix he realised that he must spend his whole life in expiation. A monk, a contemplative monk, that was it, not a country priest at all: and his peasant soul was troubled by this commandment which seemed to come direct to him from Christ. He wanted to obey his parents, to follow his uncle's example; he was the eldest of his family and had, therefore, a duty towards his brothers and sisters. He was in no position to disappear, to humble himself in this way. Thus did Benedict set up all the arguments of traditional wisdom and prudence against Christ on the cross. But Père l'Aveugle's words were like a roaring wind in his soul, and this time they were echoing the gospel, setting free the human person and the personal ideal: "Christ did not say, 'I am the conventional thing', but, 'I am the truth' . . . You will not be judged according to the customs of Paris or Poitou, but the commandments of Christian law".

Benedict's prayer was more like a battle, and the young villager wanting to fit in with the temporal order had the worst of it. The precise nature of his vocation would come to him later.

That same day the parish priest of Erin received a call from a fellow priest. Benedict laid the table, and, as was

The Library of a Priest's House

the local custom, offered the guest some gold-glinting hydromel, the ancient and favourite drink of Artois which was so cheap that even the poorest could afford it.

The visitor was giving an account of his recent journey to the Abbey of La Grande Trappe which had been reformed by Rancé in the previous century. The Curé of Erin, anxious to learn about it, drank in every word of his friend's story. Neither priest gave a thought to Benedict, who had withdrawn into a dark corner and was listening to the voice of the visitor as if it were the Voice of Fate speaking to him. Other boys of his age get this sort of sense of an inner call from reading a poem, from thinking of ships setting sail. It was curious that such a story as was told that day in the presbytery could so stir an adolescent. For the men in the story had not sought the thrilling expansion of life that youth longs for; they had narrowed their life down and bound it round with penance. It was a story of men buried alive. Yet their prayer covered the whole world like a dew rising again to heaven.

Chateaubriand was to speak of this famous abbey, whose ruins he loved so much, as "the kingdom of expiations". "The Abbey of La Trappe", he wrote, in his *Vie de Rancé,* "stands in a very lonely spot; anyone who wants to live there must bring nothing except his soul. . . ."

In his French studded with patois, this priest was saying the same thing; had he spoken in a grander style Benedict's attention might have flagged. Pictures followed each other in quick succession: the church with monks praying all night as well as all day; the fields where they worked; the refectory where every day was a day of abstinence; the chapter room where the monks made a public confession of any exterior breaking of the rule, for upon the wall was written, "Nothing defiled shall enter heaven"; the dormitories with their quilted mattresses where the monks slept fully clothed; and lastly the cemetery, where their anonymous sacrifice came to its end.

A gloomy enough set of pictures indeed, and nothing short of repulsive if the mystery we call the Communion of Saints means nothing to you. In Benedict they aroused a passionate love, and a longing to become a part of them as soon as he could. "The strictest observance, the most severe order"—his peasant reticence in words and movements went hand in hand with a leaning toward the absolute which these superlatives answered. The life led at La Trappe was geared towards the perfect purifying of the human being. Abbot de Rancé did away with adjectives in his style, as he did away with all superfluities in his life, but there is one he kept. It occurs again and again in the instructions he gave his monks: *complete* discipline, *complete* silence, *complete* renunciation. What was, in the unpruned language of the seventeenth century, completeness, became what we should call heroism. And Père l'Aveugle's Christian logic pushed to its limits had for some time been making Benedict ready to desire that completeness—that plenitude—which was to be found in Abbot de Rancé's foundation. The boy longed with everything in him to be under the influence, under the spell even, of those magnificent, hard souls who would not stop short of perfection: "It is not the man who has much who is rich", wrote de Rancé, "but the man who wants nothing. In fact, if a man were master of many worlds, his ambition would not be satisfied; every desire

The Library of a Priest's House

he had would indicate a void—he would therefore be needy. On the other hand, those who have made the apostolic gesture of renouncing the things of earth, they it is who really have abundantly, because they want nothing more, and they find in God, even in this life, a hundredfold what they have given up for love of Him".[1] It was with an apostolic gesture that Benedict silently made his formal and final choice: he was going to become a religious of the Cistercian monastery of La Trappe reformed by Abbot de Rancé. He wanted to play his part in the salvation of the world, but as yet his fears for his own salvation were too grave for his love to be perfectly pure. These moments of decision passed by unsuspected; the young have a great gift for hiding their beliefs, their doubts, their affections. The guest left without any idea what his words had meant to the student who lodged in the presbytery. He had seemed a pleasant enough youth—rather dull perhaps.

Benedict spent that evening finding the exact location of La Grande Trappe on the map. He made out his route for getting there. His listlessness at lessons became constant, and Abbé Labre spoke to him severely about it. The time for his final preparation for the priesthood was drawing near. The way he was neglecting his work might well put an end to it, might well compromise his whole future in the Church. The Curé of Erin was saying all this not as the dissatisfied teacher, but as one who understood souls, groping to find a soul's secret. He respected the intangible and mysterious element in his nephew's personality. And so Benedict, with the kind of abrupt burst of confidence typical of the naturally silent, opened

[1] Abbot de Rancé, *De la sainteté et des devoirs de la vie monastique.*

his heart to his uncle. No, he didn't think now that his vocation was to be a country priest: "I shall not remain in the world. All I want is to go away to a desert". This could so easily have been the fancy of a misanthrope, and the priest spoke against it more strongly. Most seriously he reminded his nephew of his immediate duties among his own kind. And then Benedict put a name to his desert: the Trappist Monastery of La Grande Trappe in in the diocese of Séez. Now Benedict was not strong. That, together with his bent for reading, was why his father had released him from farm work. And now—a Trappist! "You poor child", exclaimed his uncle, "you cannot know how strict that order is—it is the strictest order of all". But Benedict knew it well; that was why he had chosen it. Had he found anything stricter he would certainly have given up the idea of La Trappe. The most perfect and most difficult thing a man could do appeared to him an absolute duty. His conscience would never rest in anything less. The Curé of Erin was no dreamer. He minded more his nephew's being lured on by a mirage than the mess he was making of his Latin translations. But the good man was too human not to regret the work he had wasted; sick at heart he reproached Benedict for his ingratitude. "I did not want to hurt you", said Benedict sadly, "I fought it as long as I could". It was the language of a lover urging the strength of his love as his only excuse. There was something growing up within him, a new man whose inherited character was changing pretty considerably.

Benedict returned home. One evening, after prayers had been said, their eldest son knelt down before Jean Baptiste Labre and Anne Barbe Gransire and asked for their blessing. For these humble Christians whose every religious gesture corresponded to a belief, it was a solemn moment. And Benedict, without further ado, asked their permission to enter at La Grande Trappe. Husband and wife were dumbfounded. The parish priest occasionally talked in his sermons of emaciated monks who lived off herbs and roots. They knew about La Trappe in much the same way as they knew by hearsay about countries where missionaries risked martyrdom from savages: there was no Trappist monastery in their province. These villagers, with their deliberate minds, and the long-established customs they so easily took for granted, were afraid of anything out of the way: it was not in them to feel otherwise. But the great quality that typified them was tenacity, a silent, unreasoning tenacity. They disapproved of this extraordinary vocation, and were shocked by it in the same way as they were later to be shocked by the innovations of the Revolution. Jean Baptiste Labre and Anne Barbe Gransire sent Benedict back to his god-father, urging him to be sensible and apply himself to his work as he always had. Back in the presbytery, his uncle had bolted the door of the library in the hope that, deprived of the books which had stirred him so much, Benedict would give up this idea of becoming a monk.

Benedict complied with everything. But he found the contrast between the reasoning of his family and the terrible reasoning of God quite overwhelming. And then God Himself withdrew—or so it seemed to him. He felt as if his love was going up like a lonely flame, its brightness wasted. His prayer lost all sweetness: suffering was sanctifying it. When he said the Our Father there was no father bending lovingly over him any more, and when he said the Hail Mary there was no mother looking into the face of her child. There was a veil between him and heaven, and yet, with that clarity of vision which is the glory and the torment of youth, he was discovering the barrenness of earth. Like all those destined to a high level of mystical life, he began painfully, from ruin to ruin, to rise towards God. And Benedict was seeing his soul as we see a pane of glass in the sunshine—misted over by a thousand flaws. He went to make a general confession to a priest whose authority extended over a whole group of parishes. And for a time the absolution he received brought peace.

And then, during the summer of 1766, Erin was struck by the plague. It spread quickly in the unhealthy marshes of the Ternoise valley. The empty streets of the village stank of fever and poverty; only two shadows moved about, unwearying—Abbé François Labre, and his nephew who rang the bell that told people the Blessed Sacrament was passing them. Père Le Jeune's most terrible sermons about man's last end were nothing to the scenes Benedict was witnessing. There were saints never to be canonised dying round him who begged him to read to them from the Bible or the *Imitation of Christ;* there were also weak men and sinners: the village had its share of the proud who never thanked, never apologised, of cheats, rakes, scandal-mongering hypocrites, and above all misers, lonelier than the rest and more unhappy over the pot of gold hidden away under a stone. They all received Communion, and Père Le Jeune's sermons on the small number who are saved ceased to worry Benedict. But sins so easily forgiven seemed to flow back upon him demanding a more complete expiation. Study had

The Library of a Priest's House

disturbed him; activity brought peace. The young man who had once been inseparable from his books was now always with the sick: he never gave a thought to the contagion: physical fear would always be something quite foreign to this tortured soul. Like a Sister of Charity he did everything needed to keep them clean and neat, and did it so gently that he was scarcely noticed. He even washed the small children and combed out their matted hair. But his chief work, which he did with his uncle, was arranging for relief to be given, and devoting himself to intelligent efforts at keeping the plague under control. And the village—or what was left of it—was amazed to find in him such a spirit of initiative, and so much unsuspected common sense.

Abbé François Labre suddenly became worried over this life that was in his charge, and forbade his godson to go into the houses of the sick. And Benedict, no longer able to help *them*, bethought him of their cattle, their only wealth. He became shepherd and groom, driving the flocks out to pasture, transporting fodder on his shoulders, cleaning out cowsheds. It is curious that this saint, whose very name has become to us a synonym for dirt and slovenliness, should have worked so hard in the cause of public hygiene, as a young citizen who stood out by his courage at this calamitous time. Had Voltaire seen the good he was doing he would have congratulated him; he would have seen him as the exact opposite of the mystic with his head in the clouds. But Benedict, even when he was putting out oats for the neglected horses, still remained a mystic. Abbé François Labre had given away all his medicines, and even his own linen. One day Benedict saw that his beloved uncle too had come down

39

with the plague. He tried desperately to save his life. He fastened to the curtains of his bed copies of the Penitential Psalms, so that the priest might have them in front of him up to his last breath. Saint Augustine had wanted thus to die with words of repentance before his eyes. The Spanish Dominican, Luis of Granada—one of Benedict's favourite ascetical authors—mentions this[1]; how often were the reasons for the boy's actions to be found in his reading! Benedict, who longed for spiritual immolation, had perfect communion of charity with his uncle. For some time Abbé Labre had given up trying to turn him from the cloister: he had understood.

One September day, the Curé of Erin died. The parishioners who thought of him as their father gathered about his remains. An emaciated group of survivors, all in mourning. The singing of the Requiem was broken by sobs. Abbé François Labre had left all his goods to his godson: and Benedict sold his modest inheritance and gave the money to the poor, only keeping for himself a few books, particularly the sermons of Père l'Aveugle.

What was to become of Benedict without the godfather who had not only taught him but supported him? His father and mother never doubted that he would be a priest. They looked upon the vocation their son had come to tell them about that evening as the merest chimera. As peasants, they did not have the power to fight an idea with words, and simply acted as if they had not heard what they did not like. And Benedict, like them, found it easier to be silent than to discuss the matter. His passion had not reached its height. It was still prudently and patiently in the process of discovering itself. The

[1] *Memorial de la Vida Christiana.*

40

The Library of a Priest's House

Amettes household conferred together. Benedict must finish his studies so that he might become one of those well-instructed priests the Bishop of Boulogne called for in the Pastoral which had been read out in the pulpit. Who was to do the job? Anne Barbe Gransire suggested her half-brother, Abbé Jacques Joseph Vincent, a priest in the hamlet of Conteville, near Saint-Pol. It seemed a sensible plan. The Labre family agreed, and so did the Abbé. No path could have been smoother, no destiny more carefully fostered by the foresight of kith and kin. The paternal uncle was replaced by the maternal.

Chapter Three

Carthusian or Trappist?

WHILE Benedict was undergoing his first spiritual trials, Abbé Jacques Vincent was leading the most ascetic life imaginable in the hamlet of Conteville. His name remains alive in the religious annals of the province: he had been nicknamed the Second Saint Vincent. It was undoubtedly from him that Benedict got so absolute a passion for detachment that it became less and less frightening and more and more full of mystical poetry. Abbé Jacques Vincent would have been worthy to appear among the first companions of Francis of Assisi; his charities would have added another chapter to the *Fioretti*. Wherever he lived, the priest was often seen coming back to his presbytery, his feet bare and lacerated by brambles, after giving his shoes and stockings away to a beggar. He was even known to give up his room to the poor and go and sleep himself in a corner under the belfry—when, that is, he was not spending the whole night praying in front of the tabernacle. He was particularly good at ending the sort of village feuds in which vengeance is cherished over a quarter of a century. He

42

often rebuilt with his own hands sanctuaries that were falling into ruin. His great mercy for all living creatures even extended to old wooden statues, however mutilated and worm-eaten, when neighbouring priests had abandoned them to the wind and the weather. Abbé Vincent set himself to save them; he would bring one of them home on his shoulder, like the good shepherd carrying home a lost lamb, not because it was beautiful, but because it represented man's efforts, and the movement of man's heart towards God.

The French Revolution might persecute this refractory priest, suspect among the suspect; it might force him in his old age into an exile whence he was never to return;[1] but it could never stop him praying.

Such was the priest who took the Curé of Erin's place as Benedict's preceptor. On a December day in 1766 the young man journeyed some way out of the Ternoise valley, and came at last, by a series of uphill paths, to the hamlet of Conteville. He was then eighteen.

The presbytery where Abbé Vincent received him can still be seen today, as bare as it was then. We see it at the end of the cemetery, half hidden under a covering of thatch, moss and flowers. Having lowered your head to go in by the narrow door, you have left the twentieth century behind. It is the home of a very poor priest shortly before the Revolution. Abbé Jacques Vincent lived on a microscopic salary, plus what he got for his teaching. It was in this first room that the children learnt their alphabet and their prayers. Their faltering voices echoed against the low beams of the ceiling. The beaten earth was the only floor. A blaze lit up the vast

[1] Abbé Jacques Vincent died at Middelburg in 1794.

43

fireplace where the chain hung for the pothook. But it is the next room that conjures up best for us the austerity of the life lived there of old. Here Monsieur Vincent might be pouring out his hot soup from the sauce-pan when he suddenly remembered some misery or other in the village. He would then go at once and give away his food to someone sick, to some old soul the thought of whom had been nagging in his mind like a scruple. And so, often enough, Abbé Vincent's own meals were made up simply of bread soaked in water, and a few potatoes. On feast days, as a sign of supreme rejoicing, he would add to his menu a turnip cooked in the ashes. All his furniture he had given to the poor. And uncle and nephew would read together the Gospel texts which guaranteed their absolute poverty against whatever the morrow might bring.

"Consider the lilies of the field, they labour not, neither do they spin. . . ." When Abbé Vincent and Benedict raised their eyes, all they could see was the crosses on the tombs, stone crosses, wooden crosses, or iron crosses that swung in the wind. Whether it was snowing, or whether it was pouring with rain, they always saw these crosses; they stood between them and the rest of the world, but in the spring they were covered in wild flowers, far richer and more varied than any in the fields.

Benedict's room was no more than an attic, dimly lit by a skylight. It still contains the little desk where he used to keep his purse and his school books. The priest of Conteville did not only teach the village children: like the more roomy presbytery at Erin this poor little house also represented the first stage of a seminary. One of the boys in Abbé Vincent's charge adored playing tricks on his fellow student Benedict, whose whole youth was beset by this sort of teasing, sometimes quite cruel. Some rather clumsy rhymes, written the year he died, allude to this fact:

> Parmi ses compagnons d'école
> Il en eut de très vifs,
> Très turlupins et de parole
> Et d'humeur très actifs . . .

The child bore all this patiently: he had not yet learnt to love it. He went on with his translations and his compositions; he was acolyte to his uncle, and served his Masses. He became welded into the closely interlocking life of the hamlet with its austere joy. Whenever some scourge attacked the rural community, when disaster spread among the fields and entered the cowsheds, Abbé Vincent tolled the bell. The whole village came at once to church, and joined their pastor in saying the Miserere. Benedict added his youthful tones to their imploring voices. But even at such moments when he felt himself most strongly to be the brother of these kneeling, suffering people, he could not get away from the thought of the cloister, the thought of the desert, where, by a strange conviction that seemed to go against all the evidence, he was certain he could be of more use to mankind than by remaining among them.

The sight of some rather crude jollity that he one day chanced upon served to strengthen his determination to withdraw. The carnival at Saint-Pol, well known for being uproarious and licentious, drew crowds of peasants. And Benedict also betook himself to this nearby town, because the Forty Hours was being held in the Carmelite

Church, the largest church there. He was not going for amusement, but simply to pray. The spiritual suffering growing within him increased. Had he realised how far it could still grow, his courage might have failed him.

As he went through the small town, noisy now, later to be absolutely riotous, he looked neither to right nor left. Once across the threshold of the church, he lay prostrate. His uncle's housekeeper, who had come with him, tried several times to wrest him from his prayer. All she could manage was to make him eat a little at midday. He then returned to his contemplation as the metal to the magnet. When he finally agreed to leave the church, the noise of all the tambourines deafened him. Drunken voices bellowed out the old chorus:

> *Non, rien n'est plus fol*
> *Que le Carnaval de Saint-Pol* . . .

Harlequins, pierrots, and clowns, astrologers and fantastical gypsies elbowed each other in the streets. All charmingly dressed up, all devoting themselves to the most brutal amusements; men got up as postillions lashing passers-by with their whips; pretended wig-makers, by way of powdering girls' hair, chasing them, kissing them, and tumbling them over. Coming down the church steps, the young man witnessed some bit of licentious horseplay. And it pained him. It was not merely the madness which seized upon this Artois town for two wild days of carnival each year, and then let it fall again into the quiet of the plains around. Benedict was seeing through this to all disorder, to all sin. He made his way homeward through the crowds of masqueraders.

Like a thwarted love which will not die, the longing

for monastic life clung on. He was already foreshadowing his later wanderings, going from sanctuary to sanctuary, looking for the peace of soul that eluded him. He sought out every mission in the neighbourhood of Saint-Pol, always in the hope that some passing priest might say the word that would settle his fate, the kind of lucid and enlightening word the tortured of heart often hope to hear from strangers.

In Artois, whenever they set up a crucifixion scene a whole group of people would act out the whole Passion. Young men wearing helmets, and draped in some sort of red stuff, to look like Roman soldiers, rode along on the enormous horses of that region; with them went the cart bearing a new statue of Christ, lying on cushions: the gift, certainly, of some peasant family. And when the sad figure was nailed to the wood that lay ready for it, an old woman, much moved by the missioner's sermon, was once heard to cry: "You would think it was real!"

To Benedict Labre, who had seen such crucifixes set up in the countryside, the Passion was the one reality, the drama in which every other drama was included. For a long time Spain had owned the land where Benedict was born, where his ancestors had lived. The marks of its former dominion can still be found there—in the too-heavy magnificence of various abbey churches which bear the coat of arms of the house of Austria; in the style of building: town halls, belfries, the old bailiffs' offices; and even in the smooth brown faces of some of the people. And the realistic Sorrowful Virgins you see in Valladolid, and the Christ of the Expiation given such honour in a district of Seville, had humbler counterparts in the churches Benedict Labre visited. Did popular piety in

47

Flanders and in Artois also come under Spanish influence? It seems specially to tend towards the worship and portrayal of extreme suffering. The tiny church of Conteville was dedicated to Christ scourged at the pillar. Its expressive, rather inartistic statues impressed on Benedict's mind the thought of all the sufferings which go to make up the eternal Passion of Christ. Like the Castilian Teresa, this northern Francis wanted pictures as a material expression of his inner vision, which was already what mattered most to him.

When, in Conteville, the last of the day's works of charity were done; when the last beggar had carried off in the basket on his back the last fruits and the last vegetables Monsieur Vincent had to give, Benedict, alone with his uncle, again brought up the subject of La Trappe. Like all children whose deepest wish goes against their parents' will, Benedict found in his own family one who supported him. Abbé Jacques Vincent listened, and his loving compassion was all the greater because he too had wanted this thing to the point of agony: "I should have loved", said he, "to be poor, to have begged, to be lost to the world". Poor, begging, lost to the world: could there be a better description of Benedict Labre?

His uncle advised him to give up the thought of La Trappe which so terrified his parents. Supposing he asked their permission to be a Carthusian—he might not meet with the same refusal. Benedict welcomed this wise suggestion. Home he went to Amettes.

Abbé Jacques Vincent had judged shrewdly. The word *Carthusian* did not ring so frighteningly in his parents' hearts as did the word *Trappist*. To this fresh request

48

of their son's they agreed. There was no Trappist monastery in Artois, but several Carthusian ones. Benedict settled upon the monastery of Longuenesse, near Saint Omer.

Since their silhouette was painted for us by Van der Meulen, the French towns of the north have not changed fundamentally. There were the same fortified walls, the same clumps of steeples pointing skywards like lances carried into battle. And there were always the bells whose joyful spirits no rain or fog could damp. Carriages slowly making their way through the mud would be carrying Church dignitaries about their provinces, while the poorer religious were clattering along the rough pavements in their clogs. Artois swarmed with monks—Capuchins, Minims, Carmelites, Trinitarians—as the Revolution was to complain. And yet there was a flame that looked like going out—glowing spirituality of the kind Abbé Jacques Vincent had handed on to his nephew. Rich in treasure laid up during the ages of faith, Saint Omer included no fewer than twelve communities, and five hundred religious. Before Benedict's eyes there spread something prosperous and magnificent, but with the mark of death on it: the Abbey of Saint Bertin with its Gothic church and its immense buildings. As fast as he could, Benedict came to the Carthusian Monastery of Longuenesse, also called Chartreuse du Val de Sainte-Aldegonde, in memory of the family who founded it. It was a poor monastery, and as well known for its saintliness as for its many misfortunes. Earlier, it had been ravaged by plundering soldiers, and had just lately fallen victim to a fire, from which the damage had still to be repaired. How could they take a novice in this uncertain state? Benedict was refused—the first of many vain applications.

Priests often came to the house in Amettes, for Benedict had six priest uncles. One of them, Canon François Vincent, was stopping there when he got home from Longuenesse, and offered to take him to the Carthusians at Neuville-sous-Montreuil where he had a better chance of being taken. The travellers set off together with one horse, ridden more, one fancies, by the Canon than by the would-be Carthusian.

Legend tells how Robert VII, Comte de Boulogne, was one day venerating a picture of the Holy Face at Montreuil, when to his terror, the bloodstained face seemed to turn away from him. A flood of remorse came upon him, and all his past sins came to his mind. Deeply disturbed, he went to confide in an old Carthusian prior, who said at once: "Did you not promise to build us a monastery?" The prior's words stirred his memory, he had indeed made such a vow. And that is how, on the right bank of the Canche, facing the high-perched ramparts of Montreuil, a Carthusian monastery had long ago risen up.

Benedict Labre entered the main gate with his uncle. They were rebuilding the monastery to suit the period. The legacy of the Middle Ages was being done away with, and the monks saw without regret the disappearance of the Gothic buildings, for, as was then the fashion, they thought them ugly. Benedict read on one of the walls the peace-bringing words:

Stat crux dum volvitur orbis.

was shot through with a certain secret joy; he felt that God was confirming his own first resolve. At La Trappe, he thought, and only at La Trappe would he be given the strength he needed to overcome his weakness. The ardour of his love was never mixed with any excitement. One of his earliest teachers said of him: "He has his feet on the ground"—a wonderful quality, and one possessed by all the great mystics. Saint Teresa had her feet on the ground when she described seeing Christ and the angels with the same calm matter-of-factness she brought to making her foundations. With the same composure as Joan of Arc assured her judges: "My voices told me to", Benedict Labre said to his parents: "God does not want me to be a Carthusian but a Trappist". And Anne Barbe Gransire shivered at the sound of this word she had hoped never to hear again. Of all the children she had borne, she felt the most loving anxiety over this eldest one. Like all peasants she was frightened of anything she did not know. Her gaze was riveted on a road with no horizon, the well-worn track through the valley, already white with the first snow, the path of pedlars and tramps, and all those who passed never to return.

Once at home, Benedict practised mortifications which he took great care no one should know about. In his attic bedroom, he spent the night stretched out on a board with a log for a pillow. He was careful to tumble his bed about in the morning to conceal his asceticism. But his mother guessed. Sometimes, when she was up late at night over some household task, she would come in unsuspected. Benedict, not sleeping, would start as he heard his mother coming up the stairs. The little brass chains that held her shopkeeper's keys and scissors jangled as she walked. The poor woman was fighting for the flesh she had borne and nourished, against the spirit that was too strong for it. She upbraided him, with tears perhaps, for treating himself too harshly. And he, quite sure for himself, yet afraid of hurting his dear ones, spoke with the same shy resolve as all who have ever been in that position: "Do not worry, Mother, God is calling me to the strictest life of all. Surely I must get used to it before I start. I am getting ready to follow the ways of God".

When she heard this, her sorrow turned to anguish. God could not wish the impossible. Such rigours were not meant for young men as frail as he. And then Benedict showed the strength the will can have when it draws upon its deepest resources: "With God's help you can do whatever you really want to do. I shall live on roots like the hermits did". Benedict would certainly have found in the library of one or other presbytery the Lives of the Desert Fathers, translated by Arnauld d'Andilly. They were stories just as likely to appeal to peasants as the Port Royal letters. Up to the end of the old régime they were widely known in the country districts, and even just after the Revolution they were being read with piety by a boy who was to become Curé of Ars. They brought Benedict into contact not so much with the early Church, as, once again, with the rigourist seventeenth century in France which had dug up the long tale of penance and given it its own imprint. Anne Barbe Gransire was sister to several priests, and one wonders whether she had read the Desert Fathers. In her answer to Benedict, it seems as if the names of Hilarion, Pachomius and Macarius were not strangers to her. It was an incongruity typical of the time—this dialogue between mother and son in an Artois cottage at midnight about the solitaries of the Egyptian desert.

The austerities of the saints are frightening; but the saints themselves are not, for they are caught up in the sweetness of God. Benedict's words cut like swords, but his deep peace of soul went out like a balm to the very people he could not help wounding. His mother could not persuade him to change his resolve, or to dally in carrying it out. And yet, after these talks with him, she felt better able to face his leaving her. She had arranged for a whole group of neighbours and friends to make a solemn appeal to Benedict, but in vain. Benedict was unmoved, and Jean Baptiste Labre, whose consent was needed, gave in. He was a placid farmer, brought up on the sort of old sayings which bow to the inevitable:

> Quand le brouillard est dans la vallée
>   Pars à ta journée;
> Quand le brouillard est sur les monts,
>   Reste à ta maison.

He knew that it was just as useless to want his son to become a farmer as to sow his wheat in the wrong weather, and he was now beginning to think that Benedict would not do for the secular clergy either. Deep within him was the realisation that a vocation *must* be answered, that it was God gathering in His harvest. There are always some stooks which do not get gathered into the barns. They are the ones carried in procession when the harvest is over, and laid on the Lady Altar: they speak prayer and gratitude, and though they are never to become bread they are worth more than all the rest. As the father of many children, and as the farmer whose hands were never idle, Jean Baptiste Labre bowed before the double mystery of religious virginity and everlasting contemplation. The neighbours who criticised his eldest son must be pacified with a few rather vague catch-words: "Every soil has its own seed. . . . It all depends. . . . Let him do it his own way. . . . It's what he wants". The objections became weaker. Besides, Benedict had always most sweetly assured them that nothing could prevent his going. This resolve of his to act independently of his parents' wishes was, though not consciously, tremendous courage, for the call of his race was to him nothing more nor less than the call of the flesh, and it was being drowned by the singing of heaven. At that time fathers were used to being obeyed. Many would have thundered and stormed, like the rather too venerable old men in novels and pictures, against an eldest son who was leaving every duty to shut himself up as a Trappist. And yet, when Benedict left Amettes at the end of the year 1767, Jean Baptiste, the farmer, gave him his blessing.

One evening that same winter, in the village of Amettes, a poor wretch went down the road, so pitiable, with his shoes all torn, that the women who were fastening up their doors against burglars could not help commiserating. Benedict Labre was coming home again. He had got as far as the border between Normandy and Perche; he had crossed unending moors, great wild tracts where the snow lay over the sand. And, surrounded by lakes and woods, he found the monastery he had dreamt of ever since the first moment of his vocation, the most austere, the strictest of all. Since its reform by Rancé it had undergone no religious decline. With his own sure instinct to add to the certain knowledge he had received, Benedict felt here a most perfect centre of spirituality. But Rancé's rashness had taught his successors prudence. So many of the young monks had died of old under the austerity of the rule. Even more than at Neuville, they feared for anyone who looked quite so delicate as Benedict. The abbot—Théodore Chambon—begged him to wait a few years. They received him only as the most transient of visitors, and never gave him another thought. He came back to Artois with no notion what God wanted of him. And home in Amettes he was welcomed by a united cry of pity and of love. This return of the eldest son was an unhoped-for joy. Penitent or no, Benedict was that evening a child warming himself at his parents' fire after nearly dying of the cold.

A whole year went by. Benedict seemed to have settled down as the farm labourer he was born to be, the eldest son going out to work with his father, incredibly clumsy at this unaccustomed toil. His obedience to his father was so perfect that there were times when one might almost think he had given up the idea of La Trappe. But Anne Barbe Gransire guessed that he was as much in love as ever with a God who was asking everything of him.

Winter returned, and began in Artois with rejoicing. There were special saints to be honoured then, local saints as well as saints of the universal Church: Saint Eligius, Saint Nicholas, and Saint Catherine—in whose honour Marie-Anne, Benedict's younger sister, pinned some family brooch on her collar like any other girl who hoped one day to marry. She must certainly have felt sorry for her strange elder brother who never allowed himself any fun. As the cold weather came on, after they had killed the pig there were meals known as *tripées* or *boudinées,* followed by gatherings for rather noisy entertainment. In this household, Benedict, whom they knew so little, who only broke his silence to announce his terrifying resolves, had left the room as quietly as he always did everything. His parents, sitting in the chimney corner, suddenly grew uneasy. They well knew that their son had withdrawn to his attic to pray before his crucifix, or to re-read Père l'Aveugle's sermons.

If crises of the soul affected the soul alone, they would be simple enough; but they are all mixed up in the movement of nerves and senses. The soul of this particular young peasant had been stirred by a voice from beyond the grave. Père Le Jeune's voice, a voice far too frightening to be speaking pure Christianity. It is of the destiny of the saints that religious fear never overcomes them, but it shakes them to their roots before they reach the final rest of love. It is their trials that make them of one nature with the rest of us. And surely if we did not advert to those trials we should be turning brothers into strangers. When Christ is carving His statue, He forgets no detail for its perfection. He uses the sickness of the body as well as the suffering of mind and heart. He uses the scruples which always attack with special fierceness a soul He has chosen. The verses of the Gospel which tell us to persevere without wearying kept coming back to Benedict's mind in the form of reproaches: "Ask and it shall be given; seek and ye shall find; knock and it shall be opened to you. For whosoever asketh receiveth; and he that seeketh findeth, and to whosoever knocketh it shall be opened. . . ."

Carthusian or Trappist?

He should have tried harder, he should have found better words to convince the abbot that he had a Trappist vocation. Perhaps, if he made the same journey again in these hard winter months, the perseverance of his love would be rewarded. And bit by bit, as he sat thinking alone in his attic, he became seized by an unreasoning and impassioned decision to go back there. The snow was falling outside and clinging to the rough thatch of the roof. The landscape before him suggested to him another picture which he dwelt on mentally: "I was seeing", he said, "souls going down into the abyss, as thick and as fast as the snowflakes falling in the winter mist".

"A pure heart knows the depths of heaven and hell", we read in the *Imitation*. This innocent creature had a knowledge of sin far deeper and far more intense than even a knowledge born of experience itself. There were certain peasants living around him always in fear of bad luck and ill omens. But he, whose interior life was always uppermost, believed not in witchcraft, but in evil. To him the devil was not the evil spirit of country legend, poisoning springs and killing cattle. The spirit and the tempter Benedict feared was far too terrifying to be imagined in human form. And this spirit was more than ever at large in the world. It was his work that so many of God's creatures were rushing towards their punishment. But they were still members of the Church, of a living body, and could, therefore, still be healed. They were not fated to fall as the snow was. Benedict saw Christ on the cross, wanting to save them all, asking them to share in His crucifixion. He longed to offer himself as a victim in union with Christ. His place was among the monks who, at that very moment of the night, were praying, and by their prayer fighting against the pull of the abyss. He would return to the monastery, and this time the abbot would understand the force of his vocation.

Benedict knew what suffering this would be to his father and mother; for some time he put off telling them. But the sand in the hourglass was bearing away the days of his life, days that should have been spent in a penitential community: "See how the year is spinning by", lamented Père l'Aveugle, "and after this year, next year; and one day you will meet death". How could Benedict excuse himself to this harsh man of the seventeenth century on the ground of filial duty? The preacher would only answer: "If your father lies across the threshold of the door to prevent your going to the crucified Son of God, you must step over him". So Benedict declared to his father that his conscience was not at peace. He felt he had to go back to La Grande Trappe near Mortagne: and if they would not have him, he would go to the Abbey of Septfonts in the Bourbonnais. And, to ward off any prohibition from his father, he quoted what the preacher had said, with as much gentleness as the nature of the words would allow.

This time, when his decision became known, the whole of the village raged at him. His grandmother, who was also his godmother, came over from the farm of La Cauchiette to rebuke him. And not only his friends and his relations, but even the priest, M. Théret, reproached him bitterly. But Benedict took his reproaches with such humility, and saw so readily how fair all his reproofs were, that he was disarmed.

Carthusian or Trappist?

Public opinion has little sympathy for the unflagging effort to try again, for the slow movement of the spirit's workings. All it could see in this young man as eager to get into a monastery as the monasteries were to keep him out, was a curiosity. And Benedict, who hated singularity as pride, but was being pushed forward by this his ideal, could only answer their objections with a silence that was not the silence of consent, until his mother stepped in. She, brave woman, spoke quite calmly, without any floods of tears. She was expecting her fifteenth child. She simply asked Benedict not to leave Amettes until it was born. He agreed. In the hope of keeping him at home, Jean Baptiste and his wife asked him to be godfather to this child that was coming. Benedict knew full well the duties this would involve: he had seen enough of his own godfather's goodness to him. There is no reason to think he was any fonder of travelling than anyone else in that village, deeply rooted as they were, shut in behind their rows of trees. And yet he felt that he knew not where God might not lead him, further perhaps even than Normandy. He did not like going away, but he was going, and this time for good. How could he provide as a godfather should for the upbringing of a child who was staying in Amettes? With this as his reason, he refused. But his mother insisted, as if she claimed this as a special blessing for the life growing within her. And Benedict, meditating upon the power of prayer and upon the communion of souls in God, at length agreed.

When the primroses began to show in the orchard, the baby was born. As he had promised, Benedict stood godfather. The newborn boy was christened Augustin. He was to be the only child in the family who married and lived to old age.

There were wise priests among those who advised Benedict against becoming a Trappist. Benedict determined to seek enlightenment by making a retreat at the seminary in Boulogne-sur-Mer. He lodged in the upper town with Canon Flamand, who was from Amettes. Boulogne-sur-Mer was the scene of a great pilgrimage, the best known in northern France. It dated from a day when a trail of light had come across the sea, and a boat with neither mast, sail nor oar had sailed into the harbour, steered by angels, bearing a statue of Our Lady. The cathedral has since been rebuilt, but one can still picture Benedict prostrate there before that statue which was, in 1793, to be dressed in a revolutionary's red cap and burned.

Since Benedict was about to leave the diocese, and was still bent on entering the Trappists, he went to call at the Bishop's palace for the formality of arranging about the necessary papers. And at the same time he decided to consult the Bishop about this difficult vocation of his.

Mgr. de Partz de Pressy was one of the handful of really saintly bishops of the last years of the old régime. In the palace Benedict was coming to, the meals were frugal, the furnishing unpretentious, and the servants treated as friends. No limit was set to charity, and all the worldly goods that came in simply melted away again in alms. The Bishop was at this time fifty-seven, having been Bishop of Boulogne for twenty-five years. He lived amid heaps of books. No Frenchman of the old stock could bear seeing his faith attacked in the name of reason, the same classic and weighty reason that was his own law of thought. He had, therefore undertaken a learned refutation of Beyle and of Rousseau, but he had let alone Voltaire because, though he juggled dangerously, he was of little importance philosophically. There may have been a backgammon board lying among the scattered volumes, for the Bishop was an expert at the game; in fact a certain Englishman had heard so much of his skill that he crossed the channel simply to challenge it. History does not relate whether the Bishop won or lost, but he felt from thenceforward that he must give up any fame so worldly.

His work as Bishop was most fruitful, and certainly what was needed at the time; he fought against ignorance and gave great impetus to religious studies. In his diocese he spread the devotions to the Sacred Heart and to the exposition of the Blessed Sacrament in churches; he started the custom of ringing the church bells every Friday at the time when Christ died: generous devotions these, and destined to counteract on the one hand some of the more popular practices whose archaic flavour did not much please so educated a man, and on the other too gloomy a view of the Christian life. He never wearied of soothing and extenuating. He reduced censures and prohibitions, cases of excommunication, and the immense number of feast-days which led to more and more idleness. To make the act of faith easier, he tried, without ever swerving from orthodoxy, to temper the severity of the stricter doctrines. He had the kind of gentle nature which is pitiless only to the intolerant, and he reserved his severity for the Jansenists. He besought his priests to say nothing disheartening or discouraging in their sermons: "Never be afraid", he would say, "that there is any danger to God in appearing loving, forgiving and merciful". Bishop de Partz de Pressy was saddened by

his century and its philosophy, and yet he felt sure that
the hour of forbearance which was to save the world had
struck. He was to live long enough to welcome, after the
fourth of August, 1789, "the ending of the multitude of
burdensome constraints under which the whole countryside had been groaning". He died in a mood of optimism, just as the Revolution was dawning.

Had he known the full story of this young man who
came to him in the summer of 1769, he would have pitied
him greatly. But Benedict said nothing of his sufferings
and fears, the price he was paying for the joy he was
later to have. All he said was how intensely he wanted
to enter the Trappist abbey.

"Do your parents wish it?" asked the Bishop. He
was constantly visiting his diocese and knew this pious
Amettes family well.

Benedict was forced to admit that his parents had never
fully approved of the plan. They would still rather he
became a Carthusian at Neuville-sous-Montreuil.

"In that case, my son", concluded the Bishop, "obey
your parents. Become a Carthusian".

The Bishop spoke with such authority that it did not
occur to Benedict to mention that he had twice tried in
vain at Neuville-sous-Montreuil. With unquestioning
obedience, he resolved to try a third time.

His family were delighted; Benedict would not be
going far off: the swampy land where the monks of
Neuville worked ran down to a river whose name they
knew well. And, simple folk who hated the thought of
the irremediable, they still hoped that he might come
home again. This illusion he would not allow them: "We
shall meet again in the valley of Jehosaphat", he assured

his parents. He always said what he had to say quite
bluntly; he was not speaking proverbially; he was using
the Biblical words in their original meaning. They would
meet at the judgment seat of God. He was making an
appointment that he knew must be kept. He was leaving
the cluster of cottages, his village on earth, but not the
spiritual community that was his parish for eternity.
There was to be no separation between their souls.

On August 16, 1769, Benedict left his family. Of the
fifteen Labre children, five had died young. A much-
crossed, suffering, and very holy future awaited most of
the rest of these brothers and sisters now taking part in
the solemn farewells. Twenty years' peace, and then the
French Revolution was to overthrow all these lives em-
bedded in the old order. Some who were then little girls
were to become holy women vowed to help priest émigrés; some who were then small boys were to become
clandestine priests living in danger of their lives. In a
letter, some time later, Benedict names his brother Jacques
the second eldest, a boy of nineteen hoping to become a
priest.

As Benedict went off, the family group was splitting
up: there was little time for sorrow during the harvest.
On his way he stopped at all those chapels you find at
crossroads everywhere in Artois, and prayed to Notre
Dame des Affligés, Notre Dame de Miséricorde, and
Notre Dame de la Joie. But joy was not as yet in sight.

Chapter Four

"I Am the Way. . . ."

AT THE beginning of October a traveller came to Amettes bearing a message; he came from the Neuville monastery. Benedict had left the Carthusians, and at Montreuil-sur-Mer he had written this letter which the man pulled from his pocket. Jean Baptiste Labre and his wife read it slowly, not missing a word:

Montreuil
Oct. 2nd, 1769

My dearest Father and Mother,

This is to tell you that the Carthusians find me unsuited to their life, and that I left them on the second of October; I look on this as a command from God calling me to something more perfect still—they said themselves that it was the hand of God taking me from them. I am therefore setting out for La Trappe, where I have always so longed to go. I ask your forgiveness for all my disobedience, and for all the sorrow I have caused you. I ask both of you to give me your blessing so that Our Lord will be with me. I shall pray for you every day of my life; please do not worry about me. I wanted to stay here, but

66

they would not have me. So I am glad to be able to feel quite sure that God Almighty is leading me. Be sure you instruct my brothers and sisters carefully, especially my godson; please God I shall not cost you any more, nor cause you any more suffering: pray for me. I am very well. I gave nothing to the servants. I went to the Sacraments just before I left. We must always serve God and He will look after us; work hard to save your souls, read and follow the teachings of Père l'Aveugle: what he teaches is the way to heaven, and if you do not follow it, you have no hope of salvation; meditate on the horrors of hell which will last for eternity because of one easily committed mortal sin. Try hard to be among the few who are chosen. Thank you for all your goodness to me, for all you have done for me, God will reward you. Give my brothers and sisters the same upbringing you gave me; that is the way to make them happy in heaven; they cannot be saved unless they are taught. I promise you I shall be a burden to you no more; I have cost you much, but you may be sure that, God willing, I shall make good use of all you have done for me. Do not be distressed at my leaving the Carthusians; it is useless to struggle against the will of God who has done this for my greater good and my salvation. Please give my greetings to my brothers and sisters; give me your blessing, both of you; I will never hurt you again, and Our Lord, whom I received before I left this place, will help and direct me in this undertaking which He has inspired. I will have the fear of Him always before me, and love of Him in my heart. I have every hope of being received at La Trappe; if not, I am told that Sept-Fonts is not quite so harsh and they take people younger; but I shall certainly be received at La Trappe. I remain your respectful and humble servant,

Benedict Joseph Labre.

Saint Benedict Joseph Labre

Led by an almighty hand away from ordinary family life, Benedict pours out apologies; he repeats himself clumsily, he insists, he beseeches; he is in terror of displeasing and not being blessed. But at the same time he gives orders, and what orders they are! "Work to save your souls. . . . Meditate on the horrors of hell. . . ." Certainly a stern note on which to say goodbye to one's parents! From the bottom of their hearts Jean Baptiste and Anne Barbe blessed him. They did not criticise nor did they grumble. Their son could speak with perfect authority; he was the eldest of the family—a title in itself almost like a sort of priesthood; and he could translate Latin like a priest, and God had in fact chosen him. In the Amettes household, the advice of the absent son became the rule of life. They read aloud Père l'Aveugle's sermons. And because of the strict sense in which Père l'Aveugle interpreted every text of Scripture, Jacques Labre, Benedict's brother who was so like him, became seized with scruples, and with a terror of hell. In the evenings, they would stop their card games to listen to these old sermons as Benedict wished: "To be a saint is to be picked out, chosen, separated from the rest. To be a saint is the opposite of being an average man".

A young man who had been "picked out, chosen, separated from the rest" was at that moment trudging the roads of France. "I have every hope of being received at La Trappe", he had written to his parents. Then a couple of lines later, the probability changes into certainty: "I shall certainly be received at La Trappe". He thought only of the monastery near Mortagne. Once more he came upon that vast solitude, and once more the abbot refused to have him. This young man was going too fast; he had been told to wait longer than this. Was this impatient longing compatible with the self-denial needed of a monk? Benedict, whose only wish was to overcome all self-will, submitted: he never complained, he simply suffered.

One hope was left him: in the diocese of Autun, there was a Trappist monastery at Septfonts, where the rule allowed of taking postulants much younger. The road was long, and Benedict was poor; he could not afford the public conveyances, so went on foot from Normandy to the Bourbonnais. This long walk to the place of sacrifice is to us most moving, but if the *litterati* of the eighteenth century had heard the story, they would have thought it supremely ridiculous. As Benedict made his way from village to village, his aloofness and his whole bearing proclaiming him a monk from head to foot, the average Frenchman of the time, who prided himself on his freedom from prejudice, could look him up and down with all the disdain of the half-educated for the unrefined. And the upper classes in their red-heeled shoes and their perrukes went to the theatre to hear judgment passed on the whole idea of religious celibacy. Diderot's *Père de Famille* said to his daughter: "Nature did not give you social advantages in order to waste them. . . . Don't talk to me of convents, Miss. . . . I would not have given life to a child, nor worked untiringly to assure her happiness, if I thought she would simply bury herself—and with her the cheated hopes of myself and society". This seemed to the audience the language of nature and of truth, and they applauded it. Meanwhile Benedict was sleeping on a bundle of straw, perhaps in the barn of one of those monasteries where the communion between earth and heaven had become only a faded memory, and prayer simply a routine.

The Commission des Réguliers, set up by the King, investigated all the monasteries, suppressing those that were simply vegetating, and postponing as far as possible the age at which novices might take their vows. No time could have been less favourable for the thing Benedict wanted so passionately. So many abuses of the monastic state had sprung up, and many of the finest minds of the day delighted in identifying the folly of the cross with the folly of the imbecile. When Louis XV's daughter entered the Carmelites in 1770, Madame du Deffant wrote to Horace Walpole: "All one can do is shrug one's shoulders, pity her weakness of mind and talk of other matters". Benedict's spiritual torture was that of a man rowing against wind and tide. And as he went he blessed that nature and that life in whose name the thinkers of his day would have been condemning him. In gratitude for the hospitality given him that autumn by a vine-grower among the hills beside the Loire, Benedict made a sign of the cross over some now bare branches, and it is said that that vine became the richest of all, and was never again bitten by frost. In his poverty he was already leaving behind him a trail of miraculous traditions and kindnesses.

Two days before the Feast of All Saints he entered upon one of the long avenues that run up to the door of Septfonts. The Cistercian Abbey of Septfonts had been reformed by Dom Eustache de Beaufort, at the same time as Rancé, converted from his worldly life, was reforming La Grande Trappe. In both cases there was the same restoration of the rule, the same return to austerity. In

"I Am the Way . . ."

1769 the Monastery of Septfonts was under the governance of Dom Dorothée Jalloutz, the thirty-sixth abbot and one of the greatest. He was a man of action as well as learning; he wrote the history of the monastery, built a hospital, provided for a number of the sick poor to visit well-known watering-places like Vichy and Bourbon-Lancy. The river that ran nearby, the Bébre, did much damage by its continual flooding, and when the floods subsided they always left great sunken, unwholesome tracts of ground where fever became widespread; Dom Dorothée Jalloutz set on foot the damming of the river and draining of these swamps. He employed for the job the poor and the unemployed who thronged round the doors asking for bread. Dom Jalloutz' work-yards were in consequence known as the *Ateliers de Charité*. Once more, as the old régime with its complexity was crumbling away, Benedict was seeking for the institutions that stood untouched. He knelt in front of Dom Dorothée Jalloutz, and, in the presence of all the community, begged to be allowed to put on the religious habit. On November 11 his wish was granted. Thenceforward he was just one among the other choir novices, wearing the white woollen tunic, cloak, hood, and scapular. He was then twenty-two. No longer Benedict Joseph Labre, but Frère Urbain.

Weeks and months rolled by. A novice at Septfonts worked on the land and chanted in choir. "A good subject", his superiors said, "eager to work, and very devout". At the beginning, Brother Urbain felt great joy, and he sang his canticle of gratitude. But darkness soon followed. Just as the body feels in advance the return of an illness which has tortured it before, so his soul felt the first symptoms of this night drawing near. It was the same that had twice driven him out of the Carthusians, made as he was for light. "Let this chalice pass from me!" he begged. But the darkness closed in. In the Church nothing is wasted; everything has its place in the work of redemption: the rattle of the consumptive's cough, the blood flowing from a wound. Benedict offered the shadows that beset him to God; but God did not seem to want his offering; his prayer became paralysed. He had not imagined that any spiritual desert could be so terrible; he thought that his one love had left him. But at the same time he had a clear and desolating knowledge —the knowledge of those who have had something and have it no longer—that that love was the reason for his life, and in fact the reason for all life. With the dreadful logic of the scrupulous he convinced himself that God had rejected him: he had been thrust outside God's love, and therefore outside life. His fear of sacrilege when receiving Communion became worse and worse.

The sufferings men embrace for God borrow some of God's immensity and mystery. We know only the pale reflections of joy and sorrow, not their burning reality; the saints go to the very heart of the flame. Our moral solitudes, our secret wish for rewards, can only give us the weakest metaphors to illustrate what Brother Urbain was going through. The saints always say exactly what they mean; they are straightforward in their confessions, and because the end is triumph, their frankness comforts us: "I felt nothing but despair towards God and all His gifts", acknowledged Saint Angela of Foligno. To feel this anguish is quite the opposite of giving in to doubt.

"I Am the Way . . ."

When the temptations were worst, Benedict adored Him who allowed temptation, and willed to undergo it Himself; when the night was darkest, he knew that God's truth stood steady. Even when the suffering was most intense there was a mysterious background of obedience and security in his soul. Anguish was inseparable from faith. It was simply the finite faced with the infinite. Any love we idealise makes us feel our own wretchedness: the twofold knowledge of God and of man go to make up the ardent humility of the saints. In the darkness which was afflicting his soul, Brother Urbain saw one pinpoint of light, his conscience. A flashing gleam from a supernatural fire pierced through it, rather as sick organs can be pierced by the rays science has invented. By this merciless light Urbain saw not only his own faults and imperfections, but all weakness, all guilt, all impurity. He was crushed under the weight of sins he had not committed, and bowed under it as under the cross.

At each week's Chapter of Faults, the monks of Septfonts, as part of their routine and discipline, knelt and confessed how many times they had broken the rule. Brother Urbain could not find strong enough terms in which to condemn himself. He was expiating far more than his own sins, he was putting himself in the place of all sinful mankind who were allowing Christ's blood to be wasted. The older monks who had fought through the silent struggles to possess God that take place in the cloister, pitied this novice deeply. His suffering was no new thing to them. In language as precise as that in which scientists describe the steps of an experiment, Saint John of the Cross and many other mystics have described this darkness of soul, with its successive waves of

73

intensity, and its regular rhythm. "Have pity", begs John of the Cross, "on the soul God thrusts into this horrible and terrifying night". It is a wholly inward tragedy, but the last Act is supreme joy. It was made far worse, in Brother Urbain's case, by a subordinate, unruly drama, that of a body growing weaker all the time, and of nervous scruples which threatened to unbalance his lively mind. The Septfonts Registers state in so many words that this novice's sufferings made them fear for his reason, and that that was the chief cause for his being sent away.

In 1770, at the end of April, Benedict fell seriously ill with one of the fevers rampant in the sort of marshy land where he and his companions worked. Dom Dorothée Jalloutz came to see him in the monastery infirmary. He told him that, in order to give him the best possible care, they were going to move him to the hospice outside the enclosure for the poor and for strangers. Through the mists of his fever, Brother Urbain heard these words: "My son, God is not calling you to our order". The year before, the Carthusian prior of Neuville-sous-Montreuil, Dom Henri Cappe, had said the same thing, and Benedict was not distressed by it: he did not think himself that he was meant for a Carthusian. But if God was not calling him to the Trappists, to what was He calling him? The novice murmured: *Fiat voluntas tua.* He had left his family and his village. And now he was also being denied the silent brotherhood of the monks and all share in their supernatural and their social activities. It seemed that whenever Benedict tried to follow his vocation it was stopped up; whenever he tried to grasp it, it became far away and vague; he still had an unquenchable thirst to do expiation, but he could not yet conceive of any inde-

pendent and solitary way in which he could. Dismissed
from La Trappe, he felt more than ever forsaken by God,
encompassed by darkness. In the miserable passivity of
his illness, he knew what the darkness was for. This
night of the soul was the prelude of a brightness so
intense that it blinds before it enlightens; it was the purifying grace, the first step towards union with God. In the
depths of this night all errors were done away with, the
failings of the old man burnt away. Benedict accepted the
anguish of the darkness, and this time his abandonment
was so perfect that the darkness became lighter. He stayed
in the Septfonts hospice until July 2. His serene resignation and his prayer, monastic in its regularity, greatly
edified the brother infirmarian, who exclaimed: "This
young man is a saint!" When the time came for him to
leave, Benedict wept profusely—the comforting tears wept
by children.

Not yet fully recovered, Benedict wandered about the
Bourbonnais. One tradition has it that he was taken ill
at Paray-le-Monial. Eighty years earlier a nun had died
there whose unfortunate name, Margaret Mary Alacoque,[1]
caused smiles of irony in many a drawing room. In his
story of the parrot *Vert-Vert,* Gresset got in a dig at her.
And in the *Temple du Goût* set up by Voltaire, the mystic
was brought in as a comic gate-crasher, and at once put
out. But at home Benedict had seen a good many repre-
sentations of the Sacred Heart. The well-balanced piety
of his parents saw beyond all the crudely designed pictures and scapulars to the essence of this devotion which
the late Queen, Marie Leczinska, had done her best to
spread. A saint's spirituality never follows a system, or

[1] A boiled egg is "oeuf à la coque".

overbalances in one direction. Like all true artists who are not bound to a single school, he makes his own every spring and every flame in the Church of Christ. Benedict Labre, reader of the rigourist Père Le Jeune, was also the friend of Jesuits and honoured the memory of Marie Alacoque. Pilgrims were constantly passing through Paray-le-Monial, especially since, in 1765, Pope Clement XIII had solemnly authorised devotion to the Sacred Heart. Benedict prayed for a long time in the chapel of the Visitation Convent. A sister there, whose name has been handed on to us—Marie Constance Corbie—took pity on this poor creature worn out with fasting. Benedict was ill, and he was taken into the hospice that stood beside the Bourbince. There one nun whispered to another: "This poor man seems like a saint". They were ingenuous, simple souls, not very bright perhaps; they collected the crumbs they could find in the bottom of his wallet, and kept them as relics.

Slowly the fever left him. Though he had left Artois forever, a local expression we have already heard kept coming into his mind: *Il faut aller servir*. . . . thought Benedict. At home they thought of making a pilgrimage only at times of great trial. They said: *Il faut aller servir Saint Lambert*. . . . *Saint Josse*. . . . *Notre Dame des Ardents*. . . . *Notre Dame de Boulogne*. Benedict said with the same simplicity: *"Il faut aller servir à Rome*. I must make a pilgrimage to the tombs of the apostles". He knew not what God wanted of him, and this was the resolve that he made in his confusion; the journey once under way, light began to show through the darkness of his soul. It shone with welcoming gleams, like the lights shining through the windows of those we love which save us from dying of loneliness in a city. For Benedict, whose whole life was loneliness, the beams now piercing his darkness did not fall on faces glowing with life, or on hands ready to caress, but on skulls which had lain a-drying for centuries, on empty sockets where once had been eyes whose very gaze converted multitudes, on dust which had once been hands sowing grace in the world. There, where the martyrs had fallen; in those forests where the hermits had fasted, contemplating God; on the mountain where an archangel's sword had flashed; by the tombs of the great bishops and founders of orders; there, where the shepherd found a statue of Our Lady buried in the ground; where Christ had made Himself visible in the centre of the Host, or the blood had gushed from a profaned crucifix; in all places where matter had ever been notably dominated by spirit, the hope shone forth of miracle and of sanctification. And Benedict, like a lost child, held out his arms towards its shining. In a burst of light, he suddenly realised that his vocation was to be a pilgrim. Père Le Jeune had taught him what power relics had in driving away demons: "The lifeless bones of the saints trouble and torment those proud spirits". Benedict was quite familiar with the attacks of "those proud spirits"—he was forever being tempted, and always victorious. It would not be quite exact to say he became a pilgrim because he could not be a monk; it was because he wanted to keep the perfect integrity of a monk outside the cloister that he went venerating from shrine to shrine. He saw the saints as creatures offered in sacrifice for the love of God; and to him even these tiny scraps of their bodies had the value of consecrated offerings, which he never wearied of venerating, for he never felt pure enough.

Aller servir. . . . *Aller servir:* the Artois expression became a great inspiration that carried this man round Europe. The pilgrimage-places of his own province, even the most obscure and unimportant, revealed to him the shrines of all Christendom. Was the memory of the little chapels to Our Lady of Montserrat set up by the wayside near his home by the devotion of a Spanish soldier with him when he visited the great shrine of Catalonia? He was to "wait upon" an abbey in the heart of the Black Forest, to "wait upon" Saint Blaise whom he had always invoked at home to cure throat disease, and to the shores of the Adriatic to "wait upon" Saint Nicholas, whom Artois, like Flanders, venerated as the patron of childhood and youth.

Benedict's existence would have represented less of a spiritual tragedy had it not been based on an anachronism. When he was resolving to go to Rome, and then to Saint James at Compostella, he was not doing it as a venture: he set out with the support and approval of a priest he met on his journey, the director of a seminary, whose name we shall never know.[1] With the same total submission as he had brought to the monastic life, he now embraced the career of a pilgrim, as if it were an established way of life. As if by instinct, he rediscovered for himself the laws and statutes that had belonged to this state. The spirit of the eighteenth century had nothing in common with the spirit of pilgrimage. But a few of the ancient foundations

---

[1] Alegiani, the lawyer for the Beatification, tells us of this seminary director (*Abrégé de la Vie du serviteur de Dieu*).

were still alive. There were still, in the cities of France, brotherhoods given over to the honour of Saint Michael and Saint James; attached to every church there was always a hospice where the monks received the poor who came to visit the shrine—most of them simply tramps, though they still carried the pilgrim's shell and staff.

We find most colourful accounts of how pilgrimages had degenerated. In the reign of Louis XV, for instance, there were four Picard peasants who had amassed debts in their time of military service. More from insolvency than piety they set out for Saint James at Compostella. The most articulate of them, a man called Manier, has left us the story of their journey.[1] We see them being beaten along the roads, stealing grapes off vines, cuddling the serving maids in inns, and disturbing the sermons of the priests in Spain by their noisy mirth. And yet they were deeply moved by the famous Burgos Crucifixion: "His body was torn to bits", observed the chronicler, "you felt the blood running down before your eyes". Having got to Saint James at Compostella, they drew up a careful list of the relics there, and dutifully provided themselves from the piety stalls with "hats, shells, metal badges and the rest of the nonsense".

Benedict must have met a good deal of this rather profane merriment, but he would also have met wrongdoers fleeing their country for far more serious things than unpaid debts. The discredit quite justly attaching to these chance companions of his also touched himself, a poor beggar who could lay claim neither to a job nor a home,

---

[1] Manier, *Pélerinage d'un paysan picard à Saint-Jacques de Compostelle au commencement du dix-huitième siècle,* edited by Connauld d'Huet, Mondidier 1890.

and was therefore always in danger of the law. Pilgrims were sometimes arrested on the roads, and sent to the nearest beggars' prison. Benedict found himself lumped together with harmful and dangerous parasites, who were liable not merely to be sent to prison, but even deported; it is not altogether unthinkable that he might have ended his life of failures as a convict in the galleys. He was the type of man who always fell under police suspicion, the tramp constantly stopped with hostile requests to show his passport, often forced to spend nights in prison.

The hardships of this new life made themselves felt bit by bit. Benedict had begun to realise them on his earliest pilgrimages. And they brought back to him a scene from his childhood: he was back in the Erin presbytery, with a herd of beggars walking in the street below him; Abbé Labre's servant was shouting, "Vagabonds! . . . Lazy brutes!" Benedict was, he reflected, a beggar just like those he had pitied so much that day; priests' servants, and sometimes even the priests themselves, drove them off with broomsticks. "Vagabond!" With a shudder of inward horror which as the son of peasants proud of their hearth and home he could not help, he tried to apply the insult to himself. He said, "I am a tramp"; he would not say, "I am a pilgrim", for to be a pilgrim still brought with it some remains of honour, whereas a tramp could only provoke abuse. Benedict realised that his true destiny, his real vocation, was to be humiliated. The worst disgrace man can receive from man gives only the feeblest notion of the scorn men offered Christ. Benedict had a most accurate knowledge of Scripture. Whenever he heard someone misquote it, he would re-state the text correctly—always with great gentleness, for he hated to

contradict. And some words, above all others, from
Isaias, or from the Passion of Our Lord, expressed the
whole secret of his life, and he could not hear them
without weeping:

> Surely he hath borne our infirmities and carried our
>   sorrows:
> and we have thought him as it were a leper . . .
> He was offered because it was his own will . . .
> . . . and was reputed with the wicked. . . .
> And they did spit in his face, and buffeted him. . . .

Every Christian has the universal share of a Christian
in the heritage of Christ, but also he has his own indi-
vidual share, which is the work cut out for him to do
on earth. Those whose work is to expiate are bequeathed
Christ's Passion. And this again is divided up. Benedict
Labre's terrifying legacy was all the outrages: the blows
and the spit. That a Christian in union with the Church
has the value of a holocaust is entirely due to Christ; he
delights and glories only in his divine Mediator. Bowing
his head as the insults fell, rejoicing as passers-by stoned
him, filthy, but radiantly happy, this pilgrim was for the
rest of his life to be looked on as a madman by all except
those who could penetrate into his soul, and they trembled
in his presence as if it had been Christ in front of them.
Benedict had always wanted to live the hardest life possible. The rigours of his pilgrimages far surpassed any
Trappist mortifications; he could well have said, "My
voices did not deceive me". His rule was far too strict for
anyone else to obey. He wore the badge not of an ordinary
recluse, but of a hermit; this he was later to learn; he
still thought that although his vocation to be a pilgrim

was quite real, it was not permanent, and that some day, somewhere, he would find a monastery that would take him and keep him.

The first time a cruel child threw a pebble that gashed him Benedict felt the joy of being scorned with Christ. And his joy was only at its dawning; it had still to grow and develop. His sufferings were to be inextricably linked with a sort of strange exultation, like a Crucifixion painted on a gold background. Benedict, whom God had singled out for humiliation, would by nature have been rather arrogant; he would have set a high price on men's honour; the province he came from had once belonged to Spain, and he would have been as quick to take offence as the most sensitive Castilian.

One burning summer, and Benedict reached Italy. He had lived on charity. Harvesters, resting in the shade of hayricks, would call him over to share their dark bread with them; he would sleep sometimes out-of-doors, sometimes in cowsheds or bakehouses. In the village of Dardilly, near Lyon, one house was pointed out to him as famous for its hospitality. As he entered it, he gave the monastic greeting: "Praised be Jesus Christ", to which the inhabitants answered: "May He be praised". Benedict was given a bowl of soup, and shelter for the night. The house belonged to Pierre Vianney, a farmer with a great many children. Sixteen years later, one of these, Mathieu, was to become the father of Jean Baptiste Vianney, the future Curé of Ars, a simple soul whose ignorance and slow-wittedness almost prevented his becoming a priest, but who was to read into the depths of people's souls, and be worthy of attack by the powers of Hell. Benedict Labre

"I Am the Way . . ."

and the Curé of Ars—two spiritual brothers, separated in time by the fall of the old régime, two humiliated figures standing as a frame to the Revolution. Upon the Dardilly house, which may have reminded him of his own home in Amettes, Benedict left his sign of the cross and his prayer, which were the only marks of gratitude he could show; but they were full of such love for man redeemed by Christ, that often the sick were healed, chains of bad luck and suffering were broken, or perhaps a spiritual fire was kindled which lit up the darkness of the future.[1]

On August 31, Benedict arrived in Chieri in Piedmont. There he wrote a letter in his heavily marked script with upward sloping lines. He addressed it to a Monsieur Hazembergues, a joiner of Aire-sur-la-Lys—an uncle or a cousin one supposes—who was to deliver it to his parents:

My dearest father and mother,
     You know that I left the Abbey of Sept-Fonts, and you must be worried about what I have done since then, and what sort of life I want to take up. I am writing this to do my duty and relieve you of your worries. I must, then, tell you that I left Sept-Fonts on July 2; I still had a fever when I came away, but it had gone by the fourth day; and I set out towards Rome. I am now half way there; I have not got very far since leaving Sept-Fonts because all through August, it has been terribly hot in Piedmont, where I am; and also I was kept for three weeks, just lately, by a slight illness I had, in a hospital where I was well looked after; apart from that I have been very well since I left Sept-Fonts. There are several monasteries in Italy where the life is very regular and very austere. I

[1] Abbé Francis Trochu, in his *Vie du Curé d'Ars,* mentions a letter which Benedict is said to have written to his hosts, and the Curé of Ars to have had in his possession.

intend to enter one of these and hope God will allow me to; I have even heard of one Trappist monastery whose Abbot wrote to a French abbot saying he would receive any Frenchman who came, because he is so short of subjects; at Sept-Fonts they gave me good references; do not worry about me; I will not forget to send you news of me; I would like to hear news of you and of my brothers and sisters, but that is not possible at the moment, because I have no address. I won't forget to pray to God for you every day; please forgive me for whatever sorrow I may have caused you; please give me your blessings so that God will bless my plans; it was His Providence that directed me to undertake this journey I am now making; above all, think of your own salvation, and of bringing up my brothers and sisters; watch over what they do; think of the eternal flames of hell, and how few there are that are saved; I am very happy to be making this journey. Please give my greetings to my grandmother and grandfather, to my aunts, to my brother Jacques, to all my brothers and sisters, and to my dearest uncle; I am going to a country where travellers are well-treated; I had to frank this letter to send it to France, as I am in the King of Sardinia's territory. I will conclude by asking once more for your blessings, and your forgiveness for all the pain I have caused you.

Written in the town of Quiers in Piedmont, on August 31, 1770.

> Your very affectionate son,
> Benedict Joseph Labre.

This letter and the other I quoted are the only two of his that we have, and they are almost identical. The time between their being written was filled by the agonising noviciate at Septfonts, great physical and spiritual suffering, followed by the flash of understanding from God, the night and the dawn. None of this does he mention; there is no unburdening. "I know of one Trappist monastery . . ." he tells them. But there is no mention of its name or situation. His way of life was becoming a ceaseless journey towards a cloister that was only a mirage. The call of the road answered the call of heaven. Benedict Labre is the great patron for all who are trying to find out what they are meant to do, for he spent his life trying to find that out for himself. It may be that only in the peace of the very end did he realise that he really had found it. The way he must go was just that way of apparent instability; what was for others a means must be for him an end; he was to be a wanderer giving witness to the permanent, a messenger from eternity as transient himself on earth as the wandering Jew whose story he had heard so often as a child. Christ said, "I am the Way," making Himself, the goal of every created thing, one with the way leading to Himself, making Himself the invisible companion of those trying to find Him.

"It was God who directed me to undertake the journey I am now making". His conviction is absolute. All day long, the light of a special duty was leading him. His ancestors likened themselves to the Israelites exiled from Jerusalem, when, under Louis XIV, Prince Eugène's armies drove them from Amettes to Saint-Omer; the Labre parents were most distressed when their son wanted to leave the diocese of Boulogne. As he set off on his travels, Benedict begged the stay-at-homes in Amettes to give him their blessing. As village etiquette demanded, he sent his greetings to all, not forgetting the Canon François Henri Vincent, his dearest uncle.

In November 1770, Benedict, on his way from Loreto, venerated the tomb of Saint Francis of Assisi. Not without sidetracking and delay, he set forward for Rome. Jérôme de Lalande, who was travelling at that time, has left us a description of the small town of Assisi with its few inhabitants, its emptiness, its twenty churches, its twelve religious houses. Benedict stayed in a Franciscan friary; they gave him their badge, the rope he tied round his waist which he was to wear all his life. Benedict was drawn by special devotion to the saint who sang his happy canticle to Our Sister Death. In the low-built church in Assisi, an old painting depicts Saint Francis laying his hand on the shoulder of a skeleton, a naïve symbol for his conquered fears. Benedict with all his scruples tried to get used to the idea of death, so as to make it pleasant and familiar. He came to the neighbourhood of Assisi several times, and climbed Mount Alvernia where Saint Francis received the marks of Christ's Passion upon his flesh. When he was up there, the monks whom he begged with tears to hear his confession may have taken him for some penitent bandit, and expected some appalling tale of crime. They listened as the young man on his knees before them confessed that he had never loved God enough. All the evil in the world is less mysterious that this depth of purity.

In the steep little streets of Assisi, Benedict was given alms: his career as a mystic was beginning. The spiritual writers he read advised every Christian to become a

beggar in spirit, to make himself lower than the ground
to pray to God; Benedict Labre did more than this, he
became an actual beggar. "Man is nothingness surrounded
by God", Cardinal de Bérulle had said; and Père Le Jeune
was one of his disciples. The disciple went on: "To adore
God I should like to sink into the very centre of the earth,
the very middle of nothingness". Benedict's poverty was
intimately bound up with his virtue of religion, his fire
of adoration. By depending on his fellow-men for everything, he was admitting man's utter dependence upon his
Creator. In union with Christ who took to Himself our
humanity, he wanted, in a spirit of love, to take to himself the condition of the most abject of the poor. While,
in the course of his journeying, his body became covered
with vermin, he at first made great efforts to get rid of
it, but later, to the scandal of generations, he allowed himself to be bitten.[1] This horror sets him apart in our
memory; it puts him among the untouchables; in its
palpable reality, it still remained a symbol of mystical
abasement. More than once, the saints did things as symbols and not as examples. He looked like a medieval pilgrim, but spiritually, Benedict belonged to the seventeenth
century in France, to which the idea of the Fall was
paramount. He professed ignorance of all theology, but
had, in an unpolished state, the same theocentrism as
Cardinal de Bérulle and the great Oratorians. The scraps
of his prayers that have come down to us are simply state-
ments of the gulf between God's greatness and man's

[1] This particular penance was less astonishing to his contemporaries
than it is to us. Abbé Marconi, who was his confessor, tells us: "At
first he carefully removed them, but later he kept them for mortification". He adds, "I knew what it cost him".

nothingness: "O, God's majesty! . . . if the angels must cover their faces with their wings. . . . what will man do, who is only a worm of the earth?"

Benedict Labre was the last mystic of the old régime, which went down with one glory at least—that of having produced so many men with yearnings for the Infinite. When the pilgrim came to drink at the fountains in Umbria, he could quickly refresh his parched throat, but he could pray forever and never quench his thirst for God.

Chapter Five

Journeyings

IL MIO *corpaccio*—my carcase; that was how Benedict
spoke of his worn-out body. And yet what was his life
but an unbroken effort of that body? The peasant too
delicate for farm work, the novice who gave way under
the rigours of the cloister, journeyed on foot in the space
of seven years—from 1770 to 1777—to all the chief shrines
of Europe. He showed how far human endurance could
go by putting all his trust in God's grace. He crossed a
Europe split up into princedoms and collected a whole
bundle of different passports, German, Italian, French,
Spanish; a few of these he kept, others got lost. One described him "in pilgrim's dress". He was a type that engravings of the period often depicted. One sees the pilgrim leaning on his staff, with his money-box hanging
down at his side, resting for a moment in the middle of a
rather artificial landscape with the conventional fisher-
men and hunters passing by, a washerwoman pausing in
her work to indicate to him her sick child. Benedict Labre,
a symbol of the poor man, stands for all the poverty of
the eighteenth century. He wore an appalling old three-

89

cornered hat, and his buckled shoes were rotted with holes.

It is often only by the merest chance of a document's having been preserved, or an anecdote handed down, that we can trace his steps, and the golden legend of his life is re-woven of the finest threads. But what matter whether we know the exact length of each journey, or the number of miraculous crucifixes and Madonnas he knelt to worship? The real life-story of the man is told in his soul; his most important journey was along the road from fear to love. The day was to come when the stern man of Artois would no longer condemn. "Lent is ill-ended for those who have not kept it"—thus spoke the adolescent labelled by his mother as "severe". "When people offend God it is because they do not realise His goodness. . . . one who knows God will not sin"—thus was to speak the same Benedict, later become a man of gentleness with an infinite understanding of man's weakness. The day was to come when he would no longer tremble from a thousand scruples: "What would you do", asked one of his confessors one day to test him, "if an angel came and told you you were damned?" "I should have confidence" replied Benedict serenely.

This victory of confidence was delayed by many a falling back, many a defeat. Benedict suffered every anguish of spirit. The stories he heard as a child sometimes told of the devil dressing up as a pilgrim to deceive people; he sometimes doubted that his vocation came from God at all. With no one to comfort him, through forests where hungry wolves were howling he went, forever saying his De Profundis, his Miserere. He suffered from every yearning of the senses: though so chaste, he was tormented by impure visions; even in his rags the phantoms of pleasures he had never known sought him out to tease him. He was tempted in the same way as the hermits of Egypt whose penances he wanted to reenact. And yet with all his scruples, the fear of hell gave way by slow stages to the positive longing for heaven implied in it. In his wallet, which as the baggage of a suspicious vagrant, was constantly being ransacked, he carried his weapons for fighting despair: his books. Benedict had left the Sermons of Père l'Aveugle with his family, his own spiritual testament to them. He took with him a volume of the Spanish Dominican, Luis of Granada. We need look no further for reasons for this choice than Père Le Jeune's constant objurgations: "Read Granada . . . read Granada!" he keeps advising. "You grudge the franc it takes to buy Granada's *Memorial!*" The ardent missionary would willingly have attributed all the evils of the world to this negligence. Benedict therefore read Granada. He moved back from seventeenth-century France to six-teenth-century Spain, back to the reviving spirituality of the Counter-Reformation.

Luis of Granada's ascetical treatises were so well known in the France of Louis XIV, that Molière could slip an allusion to one of them into *Sganarelle* without surprise to his audience:

La Guide des pécheurs est encore un bon livre,
C'est là qu'en peu de temps, on apprend à bien vivre.

Benedict quite possibly knew *La Guida de Pecadores;* he certainly had the *Memorial de la Vida Christiana.* Luis of Granada is more realistic than Père Le Jeune—he might be writing a commentary on the pictures you find in Spanish monasteries; life is painted with no illusions, death is never glossed over: there are reptiles and skeletons. If you look at this book which Benedict had always with him, you can easily see why he did not scruple to treat his body as he did. He was not dirty because he knew no better; he was an ascetic of an ancient and unyielding school. "Man is born good". Just at the moment when this idea of man's fundamental goodness was becoming so widespread in Europe Benedict Labre, in some mountain path among the Alps or the Pyrenees, was reading age-old sermons about the Fall. According to Luis of Granada, man by his own nature could only say:

I am conquered by gluttony, harried by impurity, carried away by pride, my hands are bound by avarice, I am consumed with envy, devoured by uncharity, tormented by ambition, shaken by anger, numbed by laziness, discouraged by misery, yet prosperity makes me sluggish. See, Lord, what company I keep . . . see what masters I serve!

Luis of Granada pictured a world fraught with dangers, and what he advised every Christian to practise as prudence was what we would call extreme asceticism:

Virtue has no more obstinate or more dangerous enemy than our sinful flesh . . . a horsehair girdle, a small chain with a few nails sticking from it, and other things of that kind will often work wonders.

And yet this harsh Spaniard did away with Benedict's terrors. He led man down to the very depths of his own misery, and then showed him grace:

You will learn, the longer you live, that there are no places on earth where man's heart is so much at home as these: God and nothingness. In these two asylums it feels secure; elsewhere it can find nothing but torment and unrest.

Benedict, in the depths of his nothingness, was rising up towards God, becoming one with Christ. The voice of the Spanish friar was the very voice of his love, and he never wearied of it.

Familiarity is the mother of friendship with men, my brethren, and since prayer is simply an affectionate conversation with God, there can be no greater help to winning his love than often talking with Him thus . . . If a man loves perfectly, his heart will be always dwelling on his love.

As a lover is obsessed by the beloved, so Benedict lived continually in the presence of Christ, Christ dwelling within him—or, to be more precise, bowed down before the image of Christ in himself—and taking his fervour with him through the world. In the forest, he would cut down two branches and make them into a cross to carry upon his shoulder. Every mountain he climbed became a Golgotha. We tie ourselves up in narrow and painful loves; the love of this pilgrim was without limit: it embraced the whole Church, all that concerned Christ, and all that was promised to Christ. By his faith this solitary was bound up with all the universe. He was as recollected as was Saint John resting upon Our Lord's breast, and he grudged every minute taken from his adoration. What were they getting at—all those sensible, kind, and certainly well-meaning people—when they tried to suggest a cleaner shirt, less down-at-heel shoes, a more conventional hat? Benedict thanked them politely, but in the tone of an artist who is called away from his vision to be told that his tie is undone. Voltaire would not allow him to be a "man of virtue", for it was a title he refused all hermits as such, and gave, no less arbitrarily, to all who worked for the material welfare of the state, even through ostentation.[1] Benedict Labre created nothing, founded nothing, left nothing behind him but the sharp gust of his misery. His silhouette stands out best for us against desert backgrounds: the waste lands of Provence, the flat, stone-strewn ground of Castille, the sands of the Adriatic—barren enough landscapes, but they could shape a man's destiny. Benedict saw quite clearly how mad his life looked from outside: he needed all the faith he could muster to live every minute of it. "I am nothing to the world", he used to say, "I am only a useless burden on the earth; I ought to be getting ready to look at myself seriously, settling my affairs, and dying like a Christian. God grant me this grace soon!" He lived only to lose himself in God's glory. But in his passionate longing to perfect himself, Benedict enriched the whole spiritual patrimony of the world. It is souls and not actions that are apostolic; the presence of a saint always sanctifies to some extent, and no intense life of the spirit is ever wasted as far as mankind is concerned. Europe was swarming with beggars on the eve of the French Revolution. All except Benedict are now forgotten. His, like every other sublime love, looked quite use-

---

[1] "A solitary may be serious, and pious; he may wear a hair-shirt: indeed, he may be a saint . . . and if this saint were in the world, he would doubtless do much good, but as long as he is not in the world, the world is right in not calling him virtuous" (*Dictionnaire philosophique*).

less; and indeed, it could not increase God's happiness. Yet the flame that was consuming him was in fact of great benefit to his neighbours.

To the pilgrim Benedict, the man of flesh and blood was the wretched worm whom Luis of Granada and Père Le Jeune indicted so crushingly. And yet the least of men was also clothed in immense importance. He was able to offend God and be pardoned for it, to undo the whole order of creation by sin, or to merit all happiness. At home in Amettes, Benedict used to greet small children in honour of their innocence. Now, on the roads of Europe, he bowed low before travellers as wretched as himself, his brothers redeemed in Christ, over whose souls angels were battling with demons.

Acts of charity are our only landmarks in following the movingly human story of this wanderer. There are certain outstanding happenings to be noted, the *Fioretti* of a poor man who was in spirit a son of Saint Francis—tiny, unconnected events; brightly coloured, rather blurred pictures hanging in the darkness, rather like the magic lantern projections which were, at that date, drawing wondering crowds in the towns Benedict went through.

The town of Fabriano, in a valley among the Apennines, has its ancient paper works spread out along the bank of a mountain river. On this particular day—it was the end of June, 1771—heavy rain hid from view much of the landscape, with its ring of mountains, its many church towers, its tawny-coloured houses. As the storm raged, a beggar could be seen in one of the narrow streets with his wallet on his shoulder. From his rosary, one would have guessed him to be a pilgrim. A woman saw him and felt sorry for him; she called him into her house and built up the fire to dry him by.

The rain went on pattering down on the flat roofs. The poor man seemed more inclined for recollection than talk. He had asked for a needle and thread to mend his torn clothes. But so much goodness was apparent, even through his silence, that she was encouraged to chatter ceaselessly on, and her talking was choked with tears. She bemoaned the wretchedness of life in general, and her own life in particular; her visitor was forced to listen to a lengthy account of all her sufferings: she was the widow of a mason who had died by falling from some scaffolding, and she had worked her fingers to the bone to bring up her three small children, whom she intended to send abroad. She was very poor; but the pilgrim was poorer still. He finished his darning as he listened to the sorrowful tale. He heard similar at every crossroads, but to this beggar nothing that affected a human soul, a human heart or a human body could be commonplace. He said nothing specially eloquent, simply: "You must be patient", or "You must trust in God". He pronounced Italian badly. This woman he was speaking to was only an uneducated peasant; but it is the way of the simple to reach certain spiritual depths. She grasped at once that these short, hesitating, unimportant words were quite out of proportion with the peace they radiated. Some inner treachery will very often invest the words of the worldly with a hurtfulness quite beyond their meaning; and by the same kind of law the saints can use the most ordinary words and weigh them down with their own holiness. When the woman was struck down by grief, her friends had used just the same words as the pilgrim:

Journeyings

"You must be patient. You must trust in God", but they were no comfort to her at all, whereas ever since this poor creature had come into her house, she had felt a peace not of this world. So great a blessing must be shared with others. There was a girl living nearby who had had for nine years an illness no doctor could cure. The mason's widow begged the pilgrim to visit her, and he agreed to do so.

The reason for his coming to Fabriano was to venerate the tomb of Saint Romuald, founder of the Camaldolese Order. But the shrine he went to most often was a chapel dedicated to Saint James. Before the apostle's statue he renewed his vow that one day he would go to Saint James at Compostella. But he mistrusted his own impulses, and decided to consult a local priest, Father Poggetti. His name, he said, was Benedict Joseph Labre, and he told how he had wanted to be a monk, and how he had tried, and of the call from God which was now driving him about the world. What he had to say was shrewd, balanced, and clear. The priest realised that here was a genuine, deep interior life, and gave his approval to the pilgrimages Benedict had undertaken in an effort to discover what his vocation might be: he did not realise that by thus continually searching he was in fact fulfilling it. The priest watched the visitor as he prayed in the shrine of Saint James. Although hundreds of travellers stopped at Fabriano as they made on foot the pilgrimage from Rome to Loreto, he had never seen such fervour as this.

Vincenza Fiordi, a young girl living in Fabriano, lay ill. Beside her bed were pictures of Christ and His Mother; she lay where she could see the veils of the nuns

97

when they passed her window; the murmur of praying filled her sleepless hours; every waking to a new day of pain was greeted by the sound of bells. Anyone who is willing to suffer to win happiness for another is well on the way to mystical substitution, and a Christian who is concerned for his brother's soul and ready to bear the weight of his brother's sins has taken the first decisive step. Vincenza Fiordi believed firmly in exchanges between soul and soul, between heaven and earth; she believed in the communion of all men with Christ: "I am the vine, and you the branches . . ." It is the fashion of philosophers to deny the supernatural: the common people held on to the fount of holiness. To Christ's chosen sacrifice, Vincenza Fiordi added her accepted martyrdom. The sick girl, quite ignorant though she may have been, had offered her sufferings to God. But now her soul was being hard tried. All consolation had gone, and she was left with only her agony. Her two sisters, Romualda and Virginia, looked after her with the resigned devotion you sometimes find in aging spinsters. And now the mason's widow came to call on her neighbour, to tell her that the foreign pilgrim would come to see her. A sudden glow of hope for Vincenza, and a greater hope than merely the hope of being cured. At last he came as he had promised. He said, upon coming in: "Praise be to Christ". The patient and her two sisters answered in chorus, "Praise be to Him". It was the Birthday of Saint John the Baptist. They had prepared a meal for the beggar, and he agreed to have some soup, milk, and fruit, but would take very little for fear his hunger would carry him away. He would always say: "What we need is very little; all the rest goes to feed the worms". He was only at the start

of his travels: he still looked respectable, and gave no
signs of exhaustion. The Fiordi sisters described him as
having a small fair beard, *barbetta biondina,* with rather
long hair falling over his shoulders "like a Nazarene",
as speaking with the utmost courtesy, and eating not like
a common beggar at all, but with the most scrupulous
cleanliness, *pulizia*—applied to Benedict Labre, the word
is worth treasuring. He blessed the bread: "Bread is good
. . . bread is good", he repeated. As to a musician a single
chord can bring to mind the whole of a symphony, so
this bread showed him God's love for man, the cause of
every ecstasy he had, and the theme of the extempore
sermon he now gave the three sisters. "He said such
beautiful things", Virginia tells us, "that I sat listening
open-mouthed. I had never heard anything so wonderful
before". Sermons in church were never like that. "To love
God", the pilgrim explained, "you need three hearts in
one: a heart of fire for Him, a heart of flesh for your
neighbour, and a heart of bronze for yourself".

"A heart of bronze for yourself"—his deep-rooted
austerity reappeared. He was still Père Le Jeune's disciple;
hope was advancing in his soul, but had not yet won the
field. With his master, Benedict groaned over the small
number who would be saved. He gave the Fiordi sisters
a terrifying description—was it perhaps inspired by the
processions so frequent in the south?—of a procession of
penitents: some in white hoods represented the saved;
others, in red hoods, represented those who must expiate
their faults before going to heaven; and lastly, and most
numerous, those in black hoods, representing the damned.
And the pilgrim who had just been blessing God's good
bread wept as he saw this sad vision. What Christian

could sit back and rejoice in the light he saw himself, when his beloved brother remained in darkness? The Fiordi sisters were not frightened by what they heard; they declared that "the pilgrim's every sentence seemed to bring comfort from heaven". They were accustomed to being threatened from the pulpit with the most terrifying metaphors, and they could see that the French pilgrim was restrained in both his words and his gestures. By the wholeness of his faith he saw into the Infinity of mercy as into the Infinity of justice. He seems to have had, with all his downrightness, a kind of peace that was more than human.

The pilgrim spent some time in recollection before talking to the invalid. He spoke to her at length. There was some mysterious reason for Vincenza's sufferings. Was it expiation for her ancestors, or for herself, for someone she loved, or for the Church? Whatever the secret was, the pilgrim discovered it. He told her something that only she knew. Her sisters, busy about the house, had an obscure sense that the moment was a solemn one. They caught only scraps of the conversation between their sister and the stranger; they heard nothing of what was meant to remain secret. Deep in the Communion of Saints, two souls knew each other for what they were: Vincenza Fiordi the invalid, and Benedict Labre the perpetual traveller, members of the same Mystical Body, both chosen for the work of Redemption: "Courage, daughter", said the poor man, who though so young, spoke with the fatherly authority of a confessor, "for illness is a greater grace from God than health. . . . Many saints have desired to suffer the things that you suffer and have not been able to. . . . You will go from your bed straight to heaven. . . . God is calling you to some great thing, daughter. . . ."

To all appearances, it was a typical scene of the time: a pilgrim to Saint Romuald's shrine visiting someone ill. But in its deeper reality, it was a saint expressing the spiritual solidarity of all Christians: "God is calling you to some great thing, daughter". Only the faith of a saint could dare to put such a paradox to an incurable invalid tempted to despair. The very good don't so much mind not *getting* as being unable to *give;* Vincenza knew that she was serving the world: the power to love lived on unimpaired in her tortured body, and it was not fruitless: her suffering found its place in the Church's scheme of things; isolation became coöperation. She had listened to Benedict's parable: perhaps among the line of sinners in black one or other might get forgiveness thanks to her. The poor creature, given up by the doctors, wondered now at her own joy, and neighbours who had sympathised with her misery, found her smile more than they could understand. Neither Vincenza nor her sisters knew their visitor's name: "It must have been Jesus of Nazareth, or one of his saints", was all she could say.

The news soon got round Fabriano: there was a pilgrim with balm for every pain at the home of Vincenza Fiordi, the sick girl. A little girl of only ten broke out of her house and came to him; her family was rich and of some importance—*benestante*. We are not told what drama was being played out in this child's conscience. It seems that she must have put some religious difficulties to the pilgrim. They saw him discussing with her, as with an equal, he persuasive, she rebellious and eager to argue. Benedict pulled his Bible out of his bag to convince her:

"You will find the passage there"—that was the only sentence they could catch. "Although they spoke quite loudly", remarks one of the Fiordi sisters, "none of us heard what they were saying".

Mothers began bringing their children, and Benedict blessed them all: "You must love truth", he besought, laying his hand on the dark heads—many of them probably confirmed liars already!—"If you want to be like Our Lord, you must love the truth, for He was Truth itself".

Fabriano was one of the few towns where Benedict met no hatred—no little savages lying in wait at street-corners to throw stones at him. Here was nothing but veneration, and indeed he might have stayed longer at the tomb of Saint Romuald had he not noticed how popular he was becoming. Wherever he went he was followed by words of admiration: generally he did not hear, but some remark happened to break through his wall of silence, and one morning he was not to be seen: he had left before daybreak.

Each went his own way; Benedict journeyed to other shrines; the disconsolate widow found another husband; the little girl, seized so early by spiritual doubts, became a nun; Vincenza Fiordi suffered on.

Two passports, found in his wallet after his death, show that Benedict reached Naples at the beginning of 1772. That same year, he venerated the tomb of Saint Benedict in the Abbey of Monte Cassino. The Abbot of Saint Non, who had been travelling widely in southern Italy a short time before, praised the monks of Monte Cassino for their large-scale hospitality and their intel-

ligent management of their wealth. "There were very
few days on which they did not entertain two or three
hundred pilgrims, and any traveller who chose to stop
there was always received with the greatest courtesy and
kindness".[1] The Abbot also gives a description of the
miracle of Saint Januarius: the canons surrounding the
Archbishop; the casket sitting on the high altar; the
supplications of the Neapolitan crowd near to tears, and
their invectives if the miracle took too long in happening.
Strangers, like the Abbot of Saint Non, assisted at these
scenes with somewhat scornful curiosity, though they
were wise enough to smile at them, for they were mainly
artists and scholars making antiquarian pilgrimage to
Naples, to the newly discovered Herculaneum and
Pompeii. They hurried away from the cathedral and
the noisy Christians to the unruffled paganism of frescoes
and statues. But in one corner, out of all the hubbub of
rejoicing, away from all the empty credulousness, Benedict was praying on his knees.

He had not come from Rome, but from south-east
Italy. The previous autumn, he had gone down the
Ardiatic coast from Loreto to Bari, visiting every shrine
that came on the way. His link with the Franciscan order
meant that he shared all their great devotions. It is said
that Saint Francis of Assisi venerated the Archangel
Michael in the famous grotto on Monte Gargano. Tradition has it that when the Christian religion was struggling
against local idols, the Archangel took possession of that
height, and that heavenly voices came through the sea
mists singing: "It is here that God wishes to be adored".

[1] Abbé de Saint Non, *Voyage pittoresque dans les royaumes de Naples et de Sicile*.

Saint Benedict Joseph Labre

Benedict climbed upwards through the forests till he came to Saint Michael's statue and knelt among the hundreds of candles shining in the cave. He was following in the path of several holy Italians of his time, Alphonsus Liguori, Father Paul of the Cross, Gerard Majella—all of whom had come to Monte Gargano on pilgrimage to Saint Michael. From a grove of evergreen oaks, dedicated to the Archangel as so many such had once been dedicated to various gods, the monks cut small branches which they made into crosses and gave out to the pilgrims. Benedict took things of this kind most gratefully and kept them with great care. Whenever he prayed before a saint's sepulchre, he would take a few pinches of the dust away with him in a bag. Aesthetics played no part in his spiritual life. His wallet was crammed with inartistic holy cards and a hoard of cheap medals. His *Imitation of Christ* and his Luis of Granada were packed in beside booklets of no literary worth, counselling men to await death in peace. Benedict handed them out all along his route to perfectly healthy people who never gave the matter a thought. The pilgrim thought to do them a kindness by warning them most seriously that death was nearer than they thought.

When he came down from Saint Michael's mountain, Benedict set out towards the port of Bari, by way of Barletta. He became a pilgrim to Saint Nicholas. In the eleventh century, the merchants of Bari, in an effort to get ahead of the merchants of Venice, brought home the body of Saint Nicholas, which they had somehow got from Asia Minor, and their descendants had ever since been making capital out of this august booty. The wonder-worker's bones gave off a sort of balm, known sometimes as Saint Nicholas' manna, sometimes as his myrrh. It cured the sick, and the pilgrims who came all took some of it; but the whole thing was incredibly cheapened —it was even hawked about the fairs by creatures in pointed caps. Benedict, who was never troubled by any spirit of criticism, put a supply of this manna in his wallet. He thought the miraculous manna of Saint Nicholas would be good payment for the kindness of farmers who let him sleep in their bakehouses and barns.

In the church beside the Adriatic he joined in the traditional gestures of the other pilgrims, then withdrew into the all-embracing meditation that set him apart from them. When he had finished praying, his heart was full of a charity he hardly knew how to express. What, after all, did he know about Saint Nicholas, whom he had so often heard invoked at home? Fantastic stories of him were woven into scraps of popular laments: towns saved from famine, ships rescued from wreck, poor girls preserved from loss of honour, prisoners helped.

Prisoners! He suddenly saw them, as he walked through the town of Bari. Their hands were twitching against the bars of their skylight; they begged for alms, and Benedict grieved that he had none to give. The outer trappings of justice were familiar to him: from time to time he would see men in the pillory of a town square, with a notice to say why they had been put there: forgers, pickpockets, lampoonists; at the gates of towns the head of the last criminal to have been executed was sometimes to be seen withering in behind the railings. He could say in the severe tones he had learnt from Père Le Jeune: "God will judge our justice, and the virtues which give us so good an opinion of ourselves may well cause us to fear on the day of judgment, if they have been practised from self-interest or vanity, rather than charity". Were they all guilty, these prisoners? Benedict was deeply moved. And for love of them this man who fled from crowds made himself the centre of a staring circle as if he had been a comedian: peasants carrying freshly gathered olives, women balancing a pile of laundry on their heads, sailors, fishmongers, oriental pedlars. Benedict laid his hat on the ground and stuck his crucifix into the brim; he then knelt down and began to chant the Litany of Our Lady.

Tower of David ... Tower of Ivory ... Gate of Heaven ... Morning Star ... His singing cut a path through the harbour smells, the brine, the oil; its supernatural metaphors, the very essence of poetry, were like a rush of angels. All Italy at that date rang with music in honour of Our Lady. By what chance were its echoes lingering thus? The pilgrim had a mellow voice, strengthened by the habits of the cloister. As he tramped the roads he always sang French songs. The bystanders were amazed: this was moving them far more than any blind young beggar piping out love music on his flute. Why? They looked at the stranger's ragged cloak, his torn shoes mended with string. And they said, "He must be one of the pilgrims to Our Lady and Saint Nicholas, and the poor wretch can't afford to go any further". The singer came up to them. He welcomed all they gave him, and then turned to the prisoners and handed on all he had collected to them. Wherever he went, Benedict did things of this sort, and it never occurred to him that anyone might have admired him for it. The prisoners realised that his intention had been far greater than his action, and the gifts themselves pleased them less than the love behind them. Among these poor ignorant fellows, rebels, and criminals, a few were seen to weep.

His eyes on the ground, Benedict went on his way. A sudden insult echoed after him: *Gabbamondo!* Humbug! Hypocrite! A sharp stone struck him on the ankle, so that it bled. The pilgrim held his crucifix more tightly to him and prayed for his assailant. He caught a glimpse of the scamp's face—it might have been the very incarnation of hatred.

There was a famous Madonna in the village of Cossignano. Benedict stopped there to venerate it on his way to Loreto. That was in 1772. A young priest, Michael Angelo Santucci, as he was returning to the presbytery, noticed a poor man standing by the door with a rosary round his neck, holding out his hat in a gesture of begging. But the murmur from the half-opened lips was not the usual beggar's tale of woe. The priest caught a Latin phrase here and there, in an accent other than his own. The man was praying: *De profundis clamavi ad te, Domine!* . . . . Like every other cleric, he recited that psalm himself every evening, and yet he somehow felt as if he were hearing it for the first time, for never had he heard such a cry from such depths: *Fiant aures tuae intendentes ad vocem deprecationis meae.* . . . Michael Angelo Santucci watched the poor man. The absolute dregs of humanity were what usually came into the town from the pilgrims' hospice: tramps and even criminals, each with his crucifix and his rosary. But this pilgrim to Our Lady did not look like one of them. His peaceful face seemed to reflect a higher kind of peace, as if all the powers of his soul were focussed on some object worlds away from all turmoil. It was the face of a man —he did not look even twenty-five—who had fulfilled his vocation perfectly from childhood. And when the Italian priest had later to describe his pilgrim, he tried to put it into a word: *compostezza,* that wonderful completeness, that peace which the world had lost. This beggar also seemed to be a cut above the rest. The wide sleeves of his ash-grey robe fell back to disclose fine, well-made hands. And however filthy and despicable his exterior, this poor wretch who stood stranded by the presbytery door had an indefinable something about him which suggested education; or rather, there was a sort of nobility about him which went deeper than merely being civilised: *Non dico civile, ma nobile,* said Michael Angelo Santucci. With a respect he could hardly account for, the priest went up to the beggar and asked him his name, and where he came from. The query roused the man: he seemed to find it something of an effort to answer; he said with some deliberation: "Benedict . . . . French".

Now Santucci was a well-informed man, always anxious to learn more, and with a great thirst to study other languages and other peoples. With only dictionaries to help him he was then learning French, but could find out little about its pronunciation; and he at once saw in this nomad from the north a possible instructor. He must indeed have had great zeal for study, or else he felt some presentiment of blessings he was to gain from this poor man, for he invited him into his house. The Frenchman called Benedict refused at first, and it was with great reluctance that he at last gave way to the priest's insistence. Very quietly and humbly, he confessed that he was afraid of bringing the revolting insects he had upon him into the house, as it was so unpleasant for those who lived in it[1]. If this thought worried the priest, he gave no sign of it; once more he asked the poor man to come in with him.

He came several times, for Michael Angelo Santucci had arranged with the director of the hospice where Benedict was staying to let him exceed the three days the rules allowed there. And the priest was thus able to receive the desired lessons from the beggar.

Cleric and pilgrim discussed preaching in general and various preachers. Benedict spoke very warmly of the Jesuits, whose order had been suppressed by several kings and was soon to be dissolved by the Pope. Under the guidance of his unhoped-for professor, Santucci fell to reading the sermons of Father Clément, who had died the year before. Father Denis Xavier Clément had received the title of the King's preacher although he had only twice preached to the court. It was his Advent and Lenten sermons in all the main parishes of Paris that had made his name. He painted the world of his day very black, and the pilgrim, reading aloud his harsh judgments in that strong voice of his, gave rein to his own distress. Benedict wept over his country, which he saw in dreams threatened by clouds that shone blood-red. France was dying of her lust for pleasure, he would say, with an intuition he did not realise. Was she not, above all, dying of scepticism? "No, gentlemen", cried Father Clément, the King's preacher, "we cannot answer these subtle jeers, these clever satires, these sacrilegious jokes at which

[1] This is the first reference to Benedict's strange penance to be found in his Canonisation Process.

our so-called wits distinguish themselves. . . . If we try to counter their impudent sophistry with serious and sensible argument, no one even hears us: and it is safe to say that if they did, they would not listen. . . . In deep anguish, we weep as we sigh over the persecutions of the past. . . . dear God, what sort of century have you spared us for? The best of the faithful believe a faith which they do not relate to their conduct. They believe, I will not say without practising, but without thinking, without ever reflecting upon what their faith means . . . Our one wish must be to save our brethren, to become if necessary outcasts for their sake. . . ." It was pure priest speaking, in spite of the style of the orator, but he was admitting that in the intellectual field he was beaten. Against the philosophers, he was calling for mystics, victims, saints.

Michael Angelo Santucci listened to the sermons that this Frenchman, Benedict, read out with such startling earnestness. He looked rather like one of the "outcasts" the preacher desiderated. He wondered about the meaning of the bottomless humility of this tramp, who spoke about God, and Christ, His Word, in a way the priest had never heard before. Michael Angelo Santucci suspected that a mystery as old as the very notion of sacrifice had come to his house with this beggar. Benedict roused in him such a longing to be perfect that this fervent priest felt keenly his mediocrity. This poor man was the personification of faith. To think of never losing your certainty about the things of heaven! Never doubting again! Santucci was quite ready to admit to the physical disgust he felt at the dirt, at the lice. And yet he dreaded seeing his guest go, for he felt the graces of heaven would go with him. He begged him not to leave, but to stay as his servant. This he refused. In fact, he was in a hurry to be off, for the blasphemy and swearing of the other pilgrims in the hospice cut him to the quick. One morning, after serving Mass, Benedict, the Frenchman, went on his way. He gave his host a piece of paper with his name, and the name of his village and province on it; this was the greatest token he could give of his friendship.

Santucci went along with him as far as he could. When at last he left him, Benedict kissed his hand. And he retraced his steps as sorrowfully as if he had parted forever from his own brother: "I felt", he later said, "so wretched, so nearly heartbroken, that my soul seemed on the point of leaving my body; I burst into tears, and as soon as I got home, I locked myself in my room so as to weep unchecked".

The priest at Cossignano kept as a relic the bit of paper on which the tramp had written the words: "Benedict Joseph Labre, of Amettes, Artois".

During the winter of 1773, Benedict was in Moulins. He stayed there from the Epiphany till Easter, and one wonders whether the length of his stay can be accounted for by the nearness to Septfonts. Was this former Trappist novice still clinging to the hope that he might go back there? One can only guess. Special trials accompanied each visit Benedict made to the Bourbonnais. At Septfonts he had felt anguish welling up from the very depths of his soul: the monks had then cheered and comforted him; at Moulins it was a priest who caused his suffering, and he had his consolation from God.

A mason named Moret was putting Benedict up out of charity. At dawn he would betake himself to the Collegiate church—now the Cathedral—where he spent the whole day in prayer, the publican of the parable despised by nobody more than himself. With an unfriendly stare, the priest summed him up: "I thank thee, O God, that I am not as this beggar". The resemblance would certainly not have struck one. He was the Vicar-Capitular—in charge of the singers, the sacristans, and the bell-ringers. He could be seen bustling about among the ornate lecterns that held the antiphonaries. The poor man always stayed quite still at his prayer, still, and therefore, thought the priest, doing nothing, for to him all activity was visible activity. When the winter was at its bitterest, and the canons drew their fur capes more tightly round them, longing to get home to a good fire and a hot drink to soothe their throats, be it Candlemas or Ash Wednesday the poor man was sure to be there in the same place, in the same attitude. And the busy liturgist grew sick of meeting this solid block of prayer. We know nothing of him, except the function he fulfilled, and the way his dislike led him to behave on this occasion; to us he is simply a priest who had lost all memory of the things his century had put behind it.

It was after contemplating the Blessed Trinity, in the joy of something beyond reason's understanding, that Saint Vincent de Paul and his helpers, moved by a great and a practical love, set out to assist the homeless old, the orphaned young. Would it be possible to revive charity like theirs without also reviving their supreme adoration? "It is the interior life that matters", Saint Vincent would say, "hold on to that; if you fail in that, you will fail in everything". The eighteenth century had cut the old bond between mysticism and works of mercy. Only actions meant anything, or rather, only the visible part of them, not the intentions of the soul, not the buried springs gushing from its depths. "I cannot see how a virtue that does not show any result can mean anything", declared Montesquieu. The results he wanted were all material; the citizen was now to give a precise account of services rendered— the talents of the Gospel parable were outdated, with the Christian rendering to God his account of the incommensurable treasure of merits bestowed. Good and evil, robbed of all mystery, were to lose even their names: they were called the useful and the useless; writers became infatuated with these words which they found equally apt to classify men and teachings. The tutor in Rousseau's *Emile* had advised: "Only teach your children the dogmas of morality". And the most purely divine truths, the truths that made up the living heart of the faith, were dismissed as useless. Benedict Labre was purely an ascetic, he was offering himself as a sacrifice to bring these truths back into the world, in his silence he was contradicting what seemed absolutely ironclad reasoning. "What use is it? That is henceforward the most important, the determining point. . . ." the highly dogmatic tutor in *Emile* had declared. At Moulins the man who so disliked Benedict said to himself: "What use is this beggar kneeling there?" His presence irritated him in much the same way as did the statues his barbarian ancestors had built round the church doors—with their faces of ecstasy, of misery, of uncouth supplication. "Crazy, fanatical", muttered the eighteenth-century cleric. He was an official who did his job well, but Benedict had all the riches he had not. One wonders whether the whole thing could have got so much on his nerves if he had not felt some tinge of jealousy. The priest loathed Benedict for his silence; and he set himself to hunt down this unknown bundle of rags.

As Vicar-Capitular, he had rights of surveillance over the church precincts. Where did the beggar live? With Moret the master mason. Respectable people, the priest said to himself; why should they be harbouring this bothersome tramp? He went to call on Moret and find out. He learnt that the poor man's name was Benedict Joseph, that he lived incredibly frugally, eating only bits of toast soaked in water and vegetables, particularly peas. On Sunday he submitted to having two meals, which he even seasoned with a pinch of salt, and having a few dry nuts as dessert. He never gave a thought to his future; he spoke very little, but often said, "Our Lord has fed me today and He will feed me tomorrow. It honours God to trust in Him." The Vicar-Capitular shrugged his shoulders peevishly. Perhaps he envied such security. The poor man lived in an attic, where he spent a great part of the night praying. They often caught the supplication: *Miserere mei Domine!* . . . . They could tell he stayed up late from the quantity of candles he burnt. Perhaps the priest, with the quickness of his hatred, sensed in these good people a slight annoyance that so much light was being wasted: "The man is mad; one day you'll find the house on fire". And with that, the Vicar-Capitular left the house, congratulating himself on having done them a kindness. The beggar was a complete puzzle; this priest had no time for puzzles: he simply condemned. And Benedict, whose lowered eyes never missed a human reaction, sensed from the over-deliberate kindness of their actions that his hosts' feelings towards him had changed. He blessed and left them, and they did not try to stop him.

Benedict Labre was affiliated to the Franciscans, and their solidarity now helped him. A nun of their order—Sister Rivelle—took him to the house of a tailor called Fanjou, who lived with his two daughters in the Rue de la Clef. They welcomed him warmly, and they too offered him an attic; the two sisters were to cook his vegetables. He was in truth simply a Trappist who had somehow strayed into the world, and he lived by the Rule of the order he had chosen in his youth. The Vicar-Capitular carried on his investigations, busily pursuing his rounds. He knew that in Benedict's garret they had found an instrument of penance on the mattress.[1]

"Laurence, put away my hair-shirt with my discipline", he was able to quote to himself. Just as he had thought—a hypocrite. The asceticism, the fervour, it was all a show. He watched Benedict closely when he followed the procession taking the Blessed Sacrament to the sick. Such an appearance of devotion *must* be put on: he was a rogue, and utterly unworthy to walk along with the God of Majesty. This priest's soul was not very priestly; he had a professional conscience as sacristan and knew the worth of what was in his charge. Whether or not he had perfect faith in the Host, he was a most suspicious guardian of the chalices and ciboriums. There had recently been a sacrilegious theft, and the Vicar-Capitular was making ready to arrest the thief. Surely this hypocrite must be his man, this filthy beggar who pretended to be so deep

[1] This is the only mention of any instrument of penance in the Beatification Process.

in prayer to ward off suspicion. All sense of justice left him.

Now Benedict's opinion of himself was at once so low and so unruffled that no insult ever upset him. He was not above insult, but miles below it; he accepted abuse as the vain accept compliments. He could discern in himself no virtue of any sort; all he saw was the love that burnt his heart out.

It was Maundy Thursday, feast of the breaking of bread, the day when the important clerics in their ermine and purple honoured Christ by kneeling to his poor. And Benedict Labre, though he had nothing, felt in an impulse of love that the same generosity was expected of him that day as if he had been a king or the abbot of a rich monastery. The pilgrim who never made an excuse out of mere material impossibilities made his way through the town, and in no time had collected twelve beggars. They were a filthy and jeering crew, poor things, as they laughed and nudged one another at the thought that the most ragged of them all was setting himself up as their patron. Benedict led the way to his borrowed room, and their mirth increased as they saw what were the provisions he was getting ready for them: a few pennyworth of peas and some crusts. They held out their bowls derisively; and he held up his as if his few scraps were to be consecrated. And suddenly they fell silent, for he became absolutely transfigured; under his glowing fingers, the tiny pittance grew—the bowls they held were filled to the brim. The tailor's daughter breathed the word *miracle,* but Benedict simply smiled the sly peasant's smile he sometimes had, and murmured something about a generous patron who gave him everything he wanted.

Journeyings

The girl could not tell whether he meant some citizen of Moulins, or God Himself. The Vicar-Capitular was on the watch: the excitement those beggars were showing rather disturbed him. Was all his caution in vain? It was an age infatuated with occultism, and there was no lack of tricksters to exploit the naïveté of the mob. The Vicar-Capitular thought it wiser to reject where he could not explain. "I do not like the supernatural", said *Zadig*. "I have always hated the miraculous in men and in books . . ." Whatever dazzled was to him scandalous, and with more passion than logic in his reasoning, this too-reasonable priest became more and more certain that it must indeed have been Benedict who stole the prize from his sacristy: he must have shoved it into his wallet, and with that devilish dexterity of his, made off with it.

Poor Benedict's wallet contained in fact some books, and occasionally a few stones which he would put in to make it a heavier weight to carry.

One day as he was in his attic he heard moans coming from his host's room. The man was ill in bed, and his poverty made this enforced idleness a disaster. Benedict prayed; he knew that Fanjou, unlike the girl in Fabriano, did not have a vocation to suffer. After earnestly praying, he went down to where his host lay with his daughters standing in tears beside him. "Master", said he with his invariable courtesy, "this will not be serious". And the pain ceased. So Saint Peter had said—"Silver and gold I have none, but what I have I give thee".

The Vicar-Capitular went with his accusations to the tailor's house. He begged the daughters to get rid of this tramp, if only for the sake of their own good name. They objected: on Maundy Thursday he had fed twelve beggars, he had cured their father of an illness. Another miracle! And the priest had denounced Benedict to the town authorities, who would soon be arresting Benedict on a charge of sacrilegious theft. Benedict—who approached the vessels holding Christ's Body and Blood with such trembling respect—learnt what was going to happen. He had no wish either to implicate his hosts or justify himself; like a criminal escaping, he slipped away.

Benedict Labre pursued his way of humiliations, some evenings bringing him up against a cottage door, others throwing him down in sheer weariness on the steps of a large country house. In candle-lit drawing rooms, the intellectuals of society gambled away fortunes, or amused themselves in fancy dress. They rhymed what were thought to be very witty epigrams about monks, about the saints in heaven; ancient prayers were turned into madrigals: everything became a game. What heights of wit and caustic pleasantry our louse-ridden pilgrim would have called forth! Words can be oddly moulded to suit the age that uses them; at that time "enthusiasm" and "exaltation" stood for flatness: "The crusades seem to me to have been the most senseless, the most utterly *flat* enterprise anyone ever thought of", wrote Madame du Deffant to Horace Walpole. Benedict's life-story would have seemed flat indeed and his spirituality quite colourless. Painters were covering their canvases with softer and softer shades of blue and pink. Far too many doves were cooing under their unnaturally billowing clouds. The slightest hint of the pastoral was found ravishing—the mystics were tame and tasteless.

From the Bourbonnais Benedict moved on towards

Journeyings

Spain. *Aller servir.* . . . he must go to Saint James at Compostella. The vow he had made in the Chapel at Fabriano must be carried out.

As he was passing Saint-Bertrand-de-Comminges, he caught the sound of a human moan—the only sound that could ever disturb his contemplation—and he found, just at the edge of a forest, a man lying half-killed by robbers. Benedict found a stream from which to wash the open wounds, and sought in his wallet for a bit of linen to bind them: his care as a chance nurse would have challenged any antiseptic. Two horsemen came by; they saw the poor man covered in blood and were at once suspicious; they took the good Samaritan for the aggressor. The pilgrim who had come to venerate the tomb of the holy bishop Bertrand entered the town handcuffed like a criminal, dragging along behind the soldiers' horses. He was put in gaol—and it was not the only time in his life. He was also to be imprisoned at Soleure, and we do not know how many other times or in how many other places. At Saint-Bertrand-de-Comminges, the wounded man recovered to proclaim his innocence; he decided to make a pilgrimage out of gratitude, and though Benedict rarely wanted company, they set off together for Spain. When they reached Our Lady of Montserrat the stranger, having given thanks for his escape, returned on the road to Gascony, while Benedict went forward to Saragossa to the shrine of Our Lady of the Pillar. In solemn Burgos, where storks nest among the carved stone coats of arms, he bowed before the famous crucifix, the *Santisimo Cristo.* The last stage of his journey was from Santiago to Compostella. Across the centuries this solitary joined hands with all the others of his race who had made votive

119

offerings in honour of Saint James of Galicia in the churches of Artois and Picardy. We know very little about this journey of Benedict's in Spain. We have only the main features—the shocking condition of the roads, the utter weariness of the pilgrim. It may have been this weariness which made him again take a companion for his journey. He met a man called Disordino at Bilbao, who brought him as far as the Pyrenees. It was not simply that he ordinarily *happened* to be alone: out of shame he built up his own wall of isolation. On days when people thronged to the famous shrines he was to be seen outside them, ringing a little bell to warn any pilgrims who might value cleanliness to keep away from him, rather as lepers in the Middle Ages shook their rattles[1].

Numerous traditions point to his having visited Provence, and it seems likely that he went there from Spain. He probably then travelled north up the Rhone valley and came south again towards the coast[2]. He was taken in at Lunel by Saint Vincent de Paul's nuns; one district of Carpentras was called after him; he was seen kneeling praying in the areas of Arles in honour of those who were martyred there. In Aix he has had a modern imitator in the person of Germain Nouveau the poet; in Marseilles he foretold to his hosts what a great number of their descendants would become priests and religious; l'Isle-sur-Sorgue and Valréas also have memories of him, and of a certain bench he used to sit on in a thicket where he found enough shade to sleep. In Arles, Benedict, as the ragged pilgrim of the Holy Balm, brought laughter and

[1] This detail is noted in the *Vie de Benoît Joseph Labre* by a Marist father in 1882 in connection with his pilgrimage to Einsiedeln.

[2] One tradition has it that he went to Louves to venerate the tomb of Saint Francis Regis.

mockery from a group of girls; he turned round most
seriously and told the giddiest among them that she was
to enter a convent. At this their laughter became even
louder. But some years later, when she had given up her
bonnet for a nun's veil, she remembered her girlhood
and the beggar. In the mountains, Benedict was beaten
cruelly by bandits he called brothers. A barber from
Fréjus, having found him in a faint, took the pathetic
burden up in his arms and tended his wounds.

Years later, old Provençal women were still telling
their grandchildren as they came home from school with
their clothes torn, "You look like beggar Labre". As is
the custom with migrations, Benedict moved away from
the cold mists into the sun; he was the beggar of the
Mediterranean lands. The expansive always prefer to
confide their secrets in the reserved, and in Naples as in
Marseilles his silence invited people to tell him their
troubles. Benedict never went near his home province,
but he did go northwards again. The Holy Shroud of
Besançon and the incorrupt body of Saint Claude drew
him to Franche Comté. One day, as he was going along
by the Saône he heard a drowning child call for help.
Benedict jumped in the river. He had not learnt to swim,
but his faith did the work: he saved the child, and in addi-
tion, got a washing himself!

The chalets of Switzerland knew his blessing, and as
a one-time Trappist he called at the famous Cistercian and
Benedictine abbeys: Saint Urbain, Mariastein, where he
venerated Our Lady of the Stone in her grotto, and Einsiedeln among the pine forests, where pilgrims flocked.
And Benedict, who did not usually talk about his travels,
did tell one of his confessors, Father Marconi, how

particularly he loved Einsiedeln. He made his fifth visit there in 1776[1]. We do not know whether he knew the story of a certain Prince Meinrad who withdrew into the mountains there to take care of a miraculous picture of Our Lady. He had little interest in history or legend; his pilgrimages merely formed the framework for his life, the external means of attaining contemplation, the monastic discipline for curbing his body. The church of Einsiedeln was said to have been consecrated by God Himself coming in glory with his angels; it has one chapel to Saint Meinrad the hermit. Benedict knelt there in adoration of the Trinity, while the monks in their stalls chanted the Salve Regina.

We have several of Benedict's passports; he got one at Maîche in Franche Comté in 1774, when he was on the way to Constance. Another was signed in Lucerne in 1775 by the Papal nuncio. A third shows that he got to Waldshut that same year and some way into the Black Forest. These documents are all borne out by word-of-mouth tradition. Three sisters named Kromenthal in Coblentz saw him at the time, and remembered his visit so clearly that they were still talking about it in their old age to French expatriates during the Revolution. They were pious good souls, somewhat uninteresting, one gathers, and must have had precious little human happiness. Benedict's abdication of all human rights brought a glow into their emptiness. It was never the fortunate or the strong who remembered him.

And all these roads led him in the end to Rome, to the tombs of the Apostles.

[1] So Père Temple said in the Canonisation Process.

Chapter Six

The Way of the Cross at the Colosseum

CLEMENT XIV was on the papal throne when Benedict began his pilgrimages in Rome. All the Bourbon courts were intriguing to get the Pope to suppress the Jesuits. They were an order Benedict thought very highly of; he often visited their churches, often went to them for advice. Late at night on July 21, 1773 Clement XIV signed the brief *Dominus ac Redemptor,* and flung his pen away from him. The Jesuits were dissolved at last. Was Benedict's serenity shaken? Questions of policy and opportuneness were outside his scope of understanding. He continued to kiss the sands of the Colosseum and pray for martyrdom.

"This suppression will be the death of me", Clement XIV had said. And in the Jubilee year of 1775 it was a new Pope who knocked at the holy door with the traditional gold hammer. Pius VI appeared in Rome in all the majesty of his gentleness, unwrinkled, barely upon the threshold of old age, but with a fringe of white hair showing beneath his tiara. As he went through the city, decorated in his honour, his subjects shouted, *Il Papa bello! Quant'e bello!*—"How handsome he is!"

The Trinita dei Pellegrini sheltered that year more than two hundred and seventy thousand poor people all told, who had flocked to Rome for the Holy Year indulgences.[1] They sat at long tables and were waited on by the members of a certain brotherhood—mainly of the nobility—who wore flame-coloured hooded robes with masks to hide their identity. Benedict betook himself to the Hospice of Saint Louis des Français which housed the poor pilgrims from France. They were taken in there for three nights running, and then discharged, not without something in their pockets. Benedict Labre's name can be found several times on the registers. One day in the hospice he caught the sound of an Artois accent and found that it belonged to a former schoolmate, a young man named Deleforge from Nédon, the next village to Benedict's own. He too had come on pilgrimage to the Apostles' tombs, but his devotions once complete there, he was going home to Artois never to leave it again. They talked about Jean Baptiste Labre and Anne Barbe Gransire, and the pilgrim who was going back to France offered to carry any message Benedict might want to send to his parents. "What's the use of writing?" he answered —no one ever had a firmer belief in the futility of letters —"What's the use of writing? Give them my best wishes and tell them I'm quite happy".

When Benedict left the Hospice of Saint Louis he took what shelter he could find. One passer-by saw him at the

[1] Morichini, *Institutions of Public Charity in Rome.*

bottom of a pit near the Quirinale and took him at first for a large dog; he finally made out the shape of a man, a man slowly making the sign of the cross.

Benedict came to Rome for the sixth time in 1777, and made up his mind to live there. His journeyings about Europe stopped from that date. He travelled no more, except to make one journey from Rome to Loreto.

One day in 1777, an obscure painter from Lyons, André Bley, was making a sketch for one of those pictures that convents and churches order by the series, the calling of Saint Peter. Various hearty-looking tramps lounging on the steps of the Piazza di Spagna volunteered to act as his models. But he paid no heed to them; he had all the apostles he needed and was now considering what his Christ ought to look like. His eye fell upon "a young man in beggar's garb with a short red beard"; not handsome by any academic laws, and yet with a beauty peculiar to himself; and the painter, deciding to forget the conventional Christ, asked the beggar to come to his studio and pose. *Pose as Christ!* The man shuddered as if something monstrous had been suggested, shook his head and went on saying his rosary. The painter tried again, and this time the negative he got betrayed to him that the man was French; he persevered: "As a kindness to a fellow countryman?" At this Benedict was touched, and after some thought he agreed. He used often to say that charity to our neighbour should outweigh everything else. And to oblige a painter of religious subjects— a Frenchman, too—he sacrificed his horror at the notion of posing as Christ. He followed André Bley to his studio. "He came", said the painter, "posed like a statue, and refused any kind of sitter's fee".[1] From Bley's sketch a portrait was made—a peasant turned pilgrim, an ascetic face with the thickset features of a son of the soil. A mediocre, a popular picture. Two years later, a well-known artist of the day, Antonio Cavalucci,[2] came upon the same peasant as he was praying. And when he had been commissioned by the Carmelites of San Martino dei Monti to do two pictures—the Prophet Elias, and Purgatory, he felt himself drawn towards the slum streets round the Colosseum where Benedict was to be found. Extraordinary stories about him flew round from one little shop to the next. There were those who flung mud and stones at him; but there were good Romans proud to own a scrap of cloth he had worn, however dirty it might be. Cavalucci looked at Benedict with the eye of a genius and made him the incarnation of mysticism.

Surely there must have been other painters who tried to get hold of this model who posed so admirably and refused payment. If so they sought in vain; Benedict melted away and lost himself among the throng of down-and-outs.

The population of Rome at that date was about a hundred and seventy thousand. Beggars swarmed everywhere. Parasites, they overran the peristyles of the churches, and lay full-length on the flagstones—to the great disgust of all foreign visitors. When the Président de Brosses[3] came

[1] *Archives of the Foreign Ministry in Rome,* Vol. 894. Extract from a letter dated June 10, 1783, from André Bley in Rome to his brother in Paris.

[2] Antonio Cavalucci, 1752–1795, pupil of Raphael Mengs and Pompeo Battoni.

[3] A well-known minor French writer of the eighteenth century; he published a record of his trip to Italy, which was the first of a long line of travel books.

The Way of the Cross at the Colosseum

with other happy Burgundians to visit Rome in the middle of the century, he had a good many not entirely ill-humoured complaints to make against those ragged gentlemen. Had not his embroidered handkerchiefs found their way out of his pockets, and likewise his diamond-studded snuffbox? And later travellers were even more violent in attacking this scourge: "They are an unbearable vermin to other citizens, and a shame to the state", wrote Jérome de Lalande in 1776; and in that same year, Duclos noted with asperity "the swarm of pilgrims and tramps all over Italy". "There are more beggars in Rome than anywhere else", remarked President Dupaty in 1785; "they throng in from every side, and a great many of them are pilgrims".

It was a poor man's city, with bread at one bajocco a pound and meat at four.[1] And to those who could not afford even this, the monks distributed food. The majesty of the Catholic city was on display for nothing, whether one lazed about in the sun, or pursued some small unfatiguing trade, or even begged dishonest bread under the protection of the right of asylum. There was an unending stream of carriages: *Viva San Marco!* was the cry, as the Venetian Ambassador rolled by in the most glittering of them all; then there was Pius VI going past blessing the townsfolk on his way to watch the draining of the Pontine marshes which he had set on foot; then, on the eve of Saint Peter's Day, the most solemn bell-ringing of all, the delight of the lamps shining against the scarlet harnesses, the house fronts hung with flags to greet the King of Naples coming to pay his annual trib-

[1] A *bajocco* was a coin of the Papal States worth a hundredth of the old Roman crown.

Saint Benedict Joseph Labre

ute to the Pope; and on feast-days, at night, when the buildings were lit up by Bengal lights, the cupola of Saint Peter's, the Castel San Angelo shining out of the darkness.

All this enchantment was lost on Benedict, an ascetic whose eyes were always on the ground. His way of life —sign of contradiction that it was—weighed in the social scale, not on the side of the good and helpful, but as an ever-growing evil. The priests, accused of encouraging begging, thundered against it from their pulpits. Benedict took care never to ask for alms; he accepted what was given him as long as he did not think it more than he needed, but, though still only thirty, he did no work. According to one tradition, he worked as a labourer in a Provençal village. If so, this was a unique instance. At the time when all the poor of Rome were handed out soup, Benedict held out his bowl with the rest—to the Dominican sister at Saint Catherine of Siena's Convent, the Franciscan Friar at the Ara Coeli, or Cardinal Bernis' servant. The stately French cardinal lived in the Palazzo de Carolis in the Corso.[1] There was a perpetual scramble outside his door of coaches, and coachmen each bent on showing his employer's importance by letting no one else get ahead of him. The poor lined up amid the hub-bub, waiting till the steaming soup kettle was brought. And the scuffling that broke out then was not concerned with any pride of rank, but simply with degrees of hun-ger. But one beggar, bent on being the last, always held back, and seemed always detached, though one would have said his need was the greatest. And if a mother

[1] Now the Bank of Rome, opposite the Piazza San Marcello.

should come with her children too late to get any,
Benedict would give her his and disappear.

In the sweat of thy face shalt thou eat bread. . . . In
the Church of Saints Vincent and Athanasius, near the
Fountana di Trevi, Father Gabrini reminded Benedict
of this universal law. The priest was a descendant of the
tribune Cola de Rienzo; he was a professor of philosophy
and of Greek, and as a student of natural history spent
his life making a collection which he left to the Vatican
Museum; he and Père Temple of Loreto were undoubtedly the most learned of the priests who knew Benedict
well. *In the sweat of thy face shalt thou eat bread.* . . .
Benedict bowed his head: he knew he was not faithful
to this command in the Bible. Father Gabrini advised
him to look for work. He did not order it; he knew that
shortage of work rather than laziness accounted for most
of the beggars living among the ruins. "What could I
do?" asked Benedict, "I am so weak". He spoke in earnest.
Although as a pilgrim he had crossed mountains, he
knew that he had been given supernatural strength to
do it; take that away and he was left only with a body
tending towards sickness, a soul tending towards sin.
From the moment when he grasped what his vocation
was to be, he had in some strange way lost all ability to
do anything else. Gone were the aptitude and promise
that had so struck the schoolmaster in Amettes. He was
good for nothing but the cross. But, once nailed firmly
to that, clinging to Christ, driven out of self, he had a
power over his fellow-men that the greatest tyrants might
have envied. The scum of the earth became the king of
creation. It was said in Rome that even animals recog-

nised the dominion of his purity. Dangerous buffaloes, rushing headlong down the narrow streets, maddened by the shouting and goading of their drivers, would grow calm when they saw him and stand aside to let him pass.

But for any work other than contemplation, how pathetically clumsy and weak he was! "Perhaps I could wash dishes in a kitchen somewhere", he suggested to Father Gabrini. And he immediately set about carrying out this modest plan. But no cook in Rome wanted such a scullery boy. Benedict came back to the priest at Saints Vincent and Athanasius: "They all said I was too dirty and not strong enough". The priest did not press the point; instead he began questioning the beggar, to get him to disclose his soul, which he did with a kind of infused understanding of psychology that astounded the questioner. "I cannot recall without deep emotion", said Gabrini later, "how this servant of God described the great interior joy he felt at being despised by men".[1]

There was a Hospice of Santa Galla for the homeless poor. And Father Gabrini tried to indicate it to Benedict several times. But Benedict always insisted that unless the idea came to him from God, he would never change his way of life; though very docile, he wanted to be independent of any hospice, and preferred his hole. Roman charity soon found him out. It spread its net so that no suffering, no destitution, slipped through the fine-woven mesh. The government was slow and negligent, and private charity did everything: that was Rome as it had always been. There was not a beggar lying in a crevice in any temple in Rome whom the clergy did not at some time try to recruit for some work of sanctifica-

[1] Father Gabrini's report for the Canonisation Process.

The Way of the Cross at the Colosseum

tion. The fervent among them realised that a man who used his poverty to create a spiritual life was no longer a burden upon the world; far from being a parasite, he was actually helping it; however down on his luck, however degraded, he became a sacrificial victim. Did the average Roman beggar reach such heights, one wonders. They mouthed ejaculations—but prayer-words became talismans, scapulars became charms. The little metal counters they received after performing devotional exercises were bartered for the loaves they needed more. Benedict—to the amazement of the rest—kept all his; they were the medals that jingled in his wallet; and he refused to turn them to material advantage. With all the other beggars he learnt his catechism—as if a scholar were inexplicably moved by humility to study the alphabet. That was how he played his part as a powerful but hidden apostle. And one poor friend of his, Theodosio, following his lead, kept his little medals and did without the bread.

The devout among the beggars used to gather in the Forum. They visited pagan remains turned shrines, went from the Mamertine prison, where Saint Peter was, to Saints Cosmas and Damian, or Santa Maria Liberatrice. Between the Capitol and the Colosseum, the historically minded visitor was saddened at every step. There was a barber's shop under the arch of Septimus Severus; where Cicero used to thunder his orations there was now a dentist eliciting screams from his patients. On all sides were knife-grinders, blacksmiths, card-players, using the pedestals of gods' statues for their tables. *Campo vaccino* —"cow pasture"—the ruins of the Forum were well-named, for scattered flocks were cropping the grass there.

131

Saint Benedict Joseph Labre

Travellers filled their notebooks with poetic melancholy, for the same men who exalted the fruitful life and raged against celibate religious led the hymn in praise of dead stones and tombs. Benedict leant against the shaft of a column telling his beads. A traveller of impious bent might well have called to mind a few lines from Voltaire's *La Religion Naturelle* which might almost have had him in mind:

> *Penses-tu que Trajan, Marc-Aurèle et Titus,*
> *Noms chéris, noms sacrés que tu n'as jamais lus,*
> *De l'univers charmé, bienfaiteurs adorables,*
> *Sont, au fond de l'enfer, empalés par les diables,*
> *Et que tu seras, toi, de rayons couronné,*
> *D'un choeur de cherubims sans cesse environné,*
> *Pour avoir, quelque temps, chargé d'une besace,*
> *Dormi dans l'ignorance, et croupi dans la crasse?*[1]

The pilgrim moved off to join the others, and the whole procession set off for the Arch of Titus. *Ave Maria, gratia plena.* . . . They mumbled out the words mechanically. "Don't mangle your prayers", entreated Benedict. And they took the reprimand quietly from one they knew to be better than themselves. He had drunk the full bitter chalice of their shame as well as his own. They knew, these beggars, that he could see down into their conscience; but there was such mercy in the seeing that they did not mind. He always thought himself the most unworthy of all.

[1] "Do you think that Trajan, Marcus Aurelius and Titus, those adorable benefactors of an enchanted universe, whose dear and blessed names you have not even heard of, are now deep in hell with devils sticking spikes into them, while you—just because you have spent your life in squalor and ignorance holding out your pilgrim's wallet—will sit among a choir of cherubs wearing a crown of glory?"

The Way of the Cross at the Colosseum

Was it this mangling of their prayers that made the visitor to the Forum so scornful? He saw processions on every side. A flock of penitents in white, with a cross at their head, poured out of Saint Theodore's Church and followed the beggars' procession to the Arch of Titus, and the Amphitheatre of Flavian—"more desecrated by monks and rabble than anywhere else", sighed the traveller. It was time for the *Via Crucis* at the Colosseum. But then he saw a young goatherd playing the flute, just like his pagan brother sculpted in a bas-relief, and a woman strolling by with a basket of strawberries on her head, and an armful of roses. The traveller fell into a pleasant reverie, and monks and pilgrims were forgotten.

Religious Italy of the eighteenth century had been fashioned by saints, and Benedict was reaping the fruits of their apostolate. In 1750, the Colosseum, which was becoming daily a place of greater degradation, was solemnly dedicated by Benedict XIV in honour of the martyrs; and it was in that same year that the voice of the Franciscan Leonard of Port Maurice, who was to convert so many galley-slaves and mercenaries, first made itself heard. While Grignon de Montfort was at work in France, this great ascetic was preaching missions which always came to an end amid tears and sobs. Vast crucifixes threw their shadows upon the crowd. The preacher, himself wearing a crown of thorns, stirred up devotion to the Passion. Ever since Christianity began, it had been a custom for the faithful to go with Christ in spirit from the Praetorium to Golgotha; Leonard of Port Maurice, to introduce the Way of the Cross as we know it today, set up, first at his own home, Port Maurice, and later all

133

over Italy, fourteen chapels to mark the fourteen stations. And, following his idea, fourteen such chapels had been set up on the steps up to the Colosseum. One of these old Ways of the Cross that Benedict followed is still standing on the slopes of the Palatine Hill, by the road leading up to the monastery of Saint Bonaventure.

Contemporary with Leonard, another religious, Father Paul of the Cross, younger by sixteen years—he was born in 1694—was also preaching upon Christ's sufferings. He too came before his crowd with a crown of thorns pressing so deeply into his forehead that drops of blood ran down his face. With a criminal's rope round his neck, he besought sinners to repent; and he had an iron chain with which he struck his shoulders so hard that people would rush onto his platform at the risk of getting in the way of the blows and try to catch hold of his arm; and, as in the days of Savonarola, a panic-stricken mob were flinging on to a bonfire cards, dice, immoral pictures, licentious books, anything the preacher condemned.

That Holy Year, as Benedict celebrated it with the other pilgrims, Paul of the Cross died an old man. He had founded the Passionists, an order of great austerity whose object was to preach repentance to the populace.

Another order, destined to even greater expansion, was also developing at this time: the Redemptorists. Their founder, Alphonsus Liguori, did not die till after Benedict Labre. They preached God saving man. "Unless a sinner feels that God loves him", said Alphonsus, "he will not give up his sin". This apostle of mercy condemned the theatrical atmosphere of so much preaching of the day. He stopped the most terrifying of the customs, but what he kept is quite enough to astound us today. The Redemptorists kept the practice of public maceration; they held up before their audiences a dead man's skull, and quite terrifying pictures, many of them painted by Saint Alphonsus himself: Christ bleeding from every wound, souls being carried to hell by demons. They taught a doctrine of forgiveness, these missionaries, but holding aloft a torch of burning resin, they would anathematize the hardened in sin while a knell was rung in accompaniment. Those were rugged days: if men were to be shaken at all they must be shaken hard. A lash came stinging down on the back of the most ordinary criminal as he was let out of the pillory; and Christians were using the same violence that the human justice of the day demanded to satisfy the justice of God.

Expiation, "a wild and absurd notion", declared Voltaire in his *Dictionnaire Philosophique.* . . . "What possible connection can there be between the Ganges and a murder?" And what between sin and the blood of a victim? The saints of the eighteenth century upheld—sometimes in the most terrifying ways—the doctrine most widely thrown over by the world of their day, that of mystical substitution. They did not set out to humour their age. Even Alphonsus Liguori, himself—the theologian most hated by the rigourists, who composed such charming hymns at his clavichord—set out to invent a more agonising kind of hair-shirt, and beat himself unmercifully when there was famine in his diocese. His young disciple, Gerard Majella, a Redemptorist lay brother, and tailor's assistant by profession, went in for a terrifying excess of corporal punishment. He would have been taken for a madman but for his incredible apostolic power: "O God!" he cried, lacerated by his own blows, "Would that I could bring every sinner in the world back to Thee!"

But, by a contrast which throws a light on the history of Italian mysticism—and perhaps of all mysticism—these men who stuffed their mattresses with thistles and stones, approached plants and animals with Franciscan affection; their charity took on immense graciousness. Gerard Majella, as he helped travellers across mountain streams, even called upon his horse to please God together with him. They loved music and poetry, these ascetics, and burst out with poetic fire: "God's immensity creates me anew!" said Majella when young, lifted quite above earth in his prayer. And Paul of the Cross found the secrets of God's glory revealed to him in wild flowers. "Quiet, flowers, quiet", he begged, touching them gently with his stick. And at that time, too, missionaries who looked like the actors of a tragedy were spreading that most inward, that deepest devotion of all—devotion to the Sacred Heart; that devotion without which you cannot understand the full meaning of Benedict Labre's holocaust. By means of it religious Italy of the eighteenth century was able to lead to the peak of his sanctity this northerner who almost never took to any form of piety native to the south; he listened to the preaching of God's love for men—and was on fire as he listened. The rough unyieldingness of his youth was being burnt away by a mystical flame.

The memory of these famous ascetics and miracle-workers—Leonard of Port Maurice, Paul of the Cross—was still very much alive when Benedict Labre came to the Colosseum to pray.

The Way of the Cross at the Colosseum

It was the Colosseum one sees in Piranese's etchings: disorder on the grand scale, vegetation run riot; laurel bushes, brambles, junipers thrusting through every chink in the stone. In the centre of the amphitheatre, a cross; people kneeling here and there, tiny processions winding their way round; on the steps, silhouettes that might have been anything—dubious pilgrims, stage bandits. Though overlooked by a church, though placed under the care of a hermit, it was still pagan. At nightfall, its dark crevices were scenes for the lovemaking of the poorest, for the secret plotting of thieves. Priests would occasionally inspect the sanctified spot in the role of kindly policemen, but what they found could only distress them. One, a certain Aloysius Rossi, described how he circled round the amphitheatre one evening "to make sure no sin was being committed in any of the grottos".[1] The shapes he glimpsed in the half-light were not reassuring. The arcades were all swarming with vagrants, dens full of stinking humanity. And then, between two niches of lovers, he suddenly saw an odd figure: a candle-end stuck on a projecting stone lit up a deeper cavity, a sort of chapel cut into the rock; and a beggar knelt there, reciting in a low tone the night office of the monks, his spiritual brothers. "With God's help you can do anything", he had often said, "anything at all; you can even stand in the fire and not get burnt, like the three young men in the Babylonian furnace."

The priest was stunned. "The beggar of the Colosseum", he murmured, for so Benedict Labre was nicknamed throughout the neighbourhood. No one knew

---

[1] *E osservare se dentro quelle nicchie non si commetteva qualche peccato.* Statement of Aloysius Rossi.

who or what he was and the wildest guesses were made.
The most ignorant took one look at his breviary, and
thought it a Book of Sorcery. "He's a magician", the
whisper went round. Others, noticing how easily he read
Latin, the priests' language, decided that he must be
some Jesuit in hiding. Poor Jesuits—driven out of Portu-
gal and thrown on the shores of Italy—they were wandering idle and miserable all over Rome; this man might
easily be one of them. But this notion was soon dispelled.
The Latins knew Benedict was not a southerner, and
made great and generally unsuccessful efforts to find out
what he was. A Bohemian? A Hungarian? A Pole? "I
took him at first for a Pole", remarked Father Marconi,
his confessor. German, perhaps? Yes, probably German:
this seemed much the most likely idea, for a great many
Germans were at that time making pilgrimages of
penance across Europe.[1] The gossips at their spinning-
wheels wove marvellous legends of high birth for him:
"A lord . . . an important lord. . . ." "No, a prince, I am
sure", insisted the oldest and most imaginative. "Don't
you realise, he is a prince doing penance for his sins".

Underneath the fifth station of the Colosseum's *Via
Crucis*, in which Simon of Cyrene takes up the Cross
behind Our Lord, Benedict Labre lay sleeping. His bed
was a heap of straw and dried ferns. He did not sleep
long. In the middle of the night he came out into the
empty arena. The hour had struck for his most intense

---

[1] *Per me pensavo che fosse un qualche Tedesco, fissandomi su la
fisonomia forestiere, e siccome so esservi molti di quella nazione che
dandosi ad una vita penitente la seguitavano con tutto vigore, mi
figuravo che un di questi fossi il povero suddetto.* Report of a priest,
Cajetanus Reder, in the Canonisation Process.

contemplation: his prayer in the darkness, the struggle of everything in him against the evil things of the night; it was time for his solitary Way of the Cross. In spirit he was making pilgrimage to Jerusalem. A popular picture, even then touched with romantic sentimentality, shows Benedict meditating on Christ's suffering in a moonlit Colosseum. Expiation means substitution: Benedict had what his century had lost. He filled up its mystical gaps with something more than mere brotherly love, with love more analogous to the love of a mother practising most intensely the virtues her children most lacked. Why did God give Benedict the terrible gift of seeing into the consciences of others? All day long he would stand, no more than a beggar, by the doors of churches. But as people came up the steps, he could say to them: "My son, get rid of that thought. . . ." "You are undergoing a grave temptation, daughter, but God will not abandon you". He saw where those who thought themselves just were unjust, where lay the impurity of those who thought they were pure; he saw hidden deceits, secret jealousies, blind perversities, sins of the flesh committed in the spirit. Benedict Labre, the beggar, the unauthorized confessor, caused people to make the most sincere sacramental confessions of their lives. Falsehood was to him enemy number one. The falsehood when appearances belied the state of souls—"What is this crucifix doing in your room?" he would ask when he saw one at the bedhead of a thief or an adulterer; "what is it here for? Is it not there to judge the state of your home, your work and your conscience?" Men cheated when they were not just playing games, and wore disguises when they were not on the stage. Man had forgotten how to take off his mask before God.

Benedict prayed at night in the Colosseum with his arms outstretched in the mortified position he had learnt as a child in Amettes; the gesture of imploring and of protecting. He thrust himself between the glory of God and the dark stain of sin, between God's truth and all our hypocrisies. *Miserere! Miserere!* he groaned. He took all men's sins upon himself, and offered himself as a sacrifice for the salvation of the world. Love can be measured by its power of sacrifice.

The pilgrim dragged himself from one deserted station to another. Sometimes the suffering from his grazed knees, and from his legs striped with wounds which some charitable hand had bound up, became so intense that he fainted. And then he resembled another figure—the stone-carving of Christ falling under the weight of the cross. But why this need for victims of expiation? The writers of the day were posing the problem of evil in their brightest little stories, a problem they could never solve. Benedict did not explain or discuss; he simply lived.

When time came for the first Mass in the Madonna dei Monti, a church near the Colosseum, Benedict was there. One December morning, a girl parishioner, Maria Poeti, saw him kneeling on the flagstones, cleansed of all his filth and haloed in flame like Christ on Mount Thabor. She took it for an illusion caused by the rising of the sun and went out to see this dazzling day. It was still quite dark, and the only light to be seen came from lanterns hanging by the holy pictures and statues along the streets. Could that radiant being really have been this dirty beggar eating his maggoty bread?

The Way of the Cross at the Colosseum

One day, distorted and helpless, his legs hideously swollen, he was carried into a small asylum for the poor, the Hospizio Evangelico, which a charitable priest, Father Mancini, had founded near San Martino dei Monti. In his illness, Benedict's imagination, which he had not the strength to control, instinctively took him back to the Artois countryside: "There's a herb that grows at home which would cure this", he said, pointing to the tumours on his knees, "a herb that grows where I come from". An undiscovered herb in an unknown country! Benedict got better, but he had to give up his niche in the Colosseum. Father Mancini kept him as a boarder. He housed twelve poor men for a fixed length of time. But Benedict he wanted to stay permanently. If asked why he had waived his rule in favour of this particular beggar, the priest would answer that he was dealing with a saint. From the time of his admission to Father Mancini's hospice in 1779, the mystical adventure of his life took on a different aspect. He now belonged to a group. He was the colleague who, when his turn for duty came round, brought in the food and drew the water.

Rome has changed much since then, but there are a few of the poor streets well known to Benedict Labre which are the same as ever. Very early in the morning, Benedict left the hospice and made his way to a nearby church: Saint Peter in Chains, or Saint Francis of Paula, or more often the Madonna dei Monti, which is still very much the popular local church it was then. In the square beside it there is the noisy, crowded animation of the market: Benedict would pick up bits of cabbage stalk on his way through and gnaw them as he went. There are still butchers' stalls all along the Via dei Serpenti as there were in the time of Benedict's friend Zaccarelli. The Via dei Neofiti brings to mind the old College for Neophytes. Benedict used to see catechumens from all over the world pouring out of its great halls. *Adveniat regnum tuum,* he would pray with renewed hope. He used often to talk about the lands where Christ was not known.

At the beginning of the century, an apostle of the people, Lucio Filippini, who preached out of doors with a crucifix in one hand, founded an order of teaching nuns, the *Maestre Pie.* Their convent was Santa Agatha dei Gothi, and they devoted themselves to the children of the poor in their schools; little girls were taught how to read, write and work with their hands. As they sat spinning their trousseau in preparation for the day when they should marry, they could be heard singing hymns. Benedict found in their innocence much to console him for the obscene songs he heard as he went about the streets, for the anguish of hearing them sung even by children. "Do you know your Our Father and Hail Mary?" he would ask them, since they were so quick to pick up the language of vice. Later, at his Canonisation Process, the Maestre Pie had much to say in his favour; they had come to see more clearly each day what a saint he was.

Benedict's agony always began when he got to Trajan's Forum; he always knew it would be so, but he never on that account avoided it. He was obliged to cross Trajan's Forum to get to the Corso churches: "There he goes—the bigot, the hypocrite, *gabbamondo.* . . ." the cries rang out. That was the signal for the attack. All the tramps wanted to get their own back on this filthy wretch who had the crust to reproach *them* for blasphemy. The law still demanded horrible punishments for blasphemers, but more often than not the tongues of the guilty were pierced through in theory only, and, more important, justice could not get hold of them as easily as they could get hold of Benedict. "Bigot! Babbler! Cheat! Filthy brute! *Santocchio! Straccione! Pitocco! Bizzocco! Bacchettone!*" An insult came with every stone. The more violent knocked him down and battered him with blows. Some of the cruellest came from innocent-looking children. The square was deep in mud, and Trajan's column so sunk that it might have been growing out of a well of mire. There were always plenty of young artists copying the bas-reliefs, but why should such an incident among the crowd disturb them? A merciless rabble setting upon some sort of begging monk—it was all part of the ugliness one shut one's eyes to. It was only a few poor women who saw what Benedict was doing: he was kissing the stones spattered with his own blood. A Venetian, Maria Clara Donati, called out to the attackers: "He isn't a madman—he's a saint!" Two almost identical churches, both dedicated to Our Lady, stood in the square: the Madonna de Loreto with the guild hospice of the bakers beside it, and the recently built Holy Name of Mary. Benedict's martyrdom ended only when he attained one or other place of sanctuary. He, who was so afraid of having too much that he often went without what he actually needed, used to pray in churches where ornamentation ran riot, under cupolas which masters of perspective had covered in sturdily built angels, brimming wth joyous vitality. Benedict was nicknamed the Beggar of the Quarantore. Wherever the Blessed Sacrament was exposed he was to be found. Did

his rags attract more attention in smarter neighbour-
hoods? He was often reported at the Gesu, at San Marcello, at the Holy Apostles, at San Andrea delle Valle,
at San Ignacio.

Sometimes Benedict would be thrown into an absolute
ecstasy by simply contemplating a picture—however little
its artistic worth. Thus with some painting, not known
to us, of the Prodigal Son; thus with the large picture
that still hangs over the high altar at San Ignacio. It
shows Christ appearing above the clouds, carrying his
cross, and Saint Ignatius bending low as if to receive it
from Him: "Give me your cross", begged Benedict, "Give
it to me!" He wanted to suffer all the sorrow in the world;
he offered every fibre of his being for the Redemption,
and besought God to spare other people who did not thus
belong wholly to sacrifice, but to the ordinary work of
the world. At moments like this, the same spirit that
seized Saint Teresa and Saint John of the Cross took
hold of Benedict, and his body followed the movement
of his soul. "What is happening to him?" Some terrified
worshipper ran to the sacristan: Benedict seemed lifted
above the ground in a position that defied all laws of
weight and balance. But the sacristan did not turn a
hair: "The saint is in ecstasy", he answered calmly, and
went on sweeping the floor.[1]

If Piranese painted for us the ruins where Benedict
took shelter, it is a lesser artist, Pannini, who depicted
for us in all its detail the pageant of Roman churches.
There were the hordes of poor people licking the stone

[1] A great many of the Italians called in for the Beatification Process
spoke of Benedict's ecstasies, and the phenomenon of levitation that
went with them. It was the Franciscan, Arbusti, who recorded the
ecstasy in front of the high altar at San Ignacio.

The Way of the Cross at the Colosseum

floor: this was a practice recommended by certain preachers as a reparation for blasphemy. (And *how* Benedict disliked these absurd prostrations! "What good does it do?" he would sigh.) And there were the social butterflies walking in and out among the colonnades on the arms of their cavaliers. And then there was music to add charm to these silhouettes. The well-harmonised notes of harps, flutes, violins and mandolins drew an enthusiastic *bravo* from the worshipper, and a *bravissimo* from the stranger polite enough to outdo him. It distressed Benedict that there was so little silence in the churches in the capital city of the Christian world. Père Le Jeune was harsh in condemning "people who bring dogs into church, who bring children, who walk about, and who make love". Benedict Labre blessed the children, but would sometimes gently propel some of the little dogs that yapped on all sides out of the sacred building. And then the owners of those dogs would fall with their sticks upon this wretched creature who dared to put out animals far cleaner than he. Insulted, thrashed unmercifully, pushed by a servant out of the way of his patrician mistress who swept by with her veil down, Benedict pursued his circuit of churches. Sometimes under a portico he would meet his friend George Zitli, an aged oriental, and together they would seek silence.

They had first met in a village in the Apennines. Zitli was going from Rome to Loreto, Benedict returning from Loreto to Rome. The old man was moved to pity by the weariness of the young pilgrim, and invited Benedict to share his meal at the nearby inn. Benedict usually kept away from inns—he did not say "Because I am too poor", for he knew he could always hope for charity; he said instead, "God is too often offended in inns". However, this time he accepted the traveller's offer. He learnt that he came from Persia, and had been born in Ispahan. Benedict did not exclaim, "How terrible to be a Persian!", but simply concluded sadly, "Then you are not a Christian". According to his spiritual geography, Persia with its sun-worship was in the area of shadow. But the old man reassured him; Christ's truth had won him over. And this so delighted Benedict that he paid but little attention as Zitli the Oriental told his story: he had formerly been treasurer to the Shah Nadir, a most bloodthirsty character. The Shah had attained the height of his power by cutting his uncle's throat; and he kept it by such violent measures as having his eldest son's eyes gouged out; he had at last died, being—suitably enough —assassinated by one of his own guards at the instigation of his nephew. How true could it be to say, Like master, like man? Benedict's companion might well cause anxiety on this score. And yet he was gentle and recollected now, sitting beneath the vine arbour of the inn, even though he had been involved—perhaps even personally—in so many massacres. Though now in his eighties, he was still a pilgrim expiating his errors and his crimes. "And you are now a Christian", Benedict kept repeating joyfully, "and you are now a Christian". A man had found the cross among cities in ruin, among palaces on fire; one with Christ, he had passed from death into life. "And now you are a Christian!" When they parted, like monks who, possessing nothing, express their friendship by an exchange of exactly similar officebooks, these two pilgrims promised each other a prayer: "Say a Hail Mary to Our Lady of Loreto", begged Bene-

The Way of the Cross at the Colosseum

dict. "Say an Our Father for me at Saint Peter's when you get to Rome", replied Zitli. And they set off in their opposite directions. That afternoon, as Zitli relaxed in the pleasant drowsiness of a siesta, he overheard two peasant women talking: "Your baby isn't crying at all today", said one, "and he was so sick yesterday". "He nearly died", replied the mother, "but a pilgrim who was going by cured him. He was young and pale with a sort of ash-coloured hood—the poorest pilgrim I've ever seen. He prayed for a long time and then told me the baby would get better".

When the oriental returned to Rome, where the Capuchins in their charity gave him a home, he met his fellow-traveller again, and tried to kiss the hand that had healed. But Benedict was annoyed by any mark of esteem shown him; all homage must go to God. The old man understood and the friends communed in prayer and silence. On the steps in front of the Trinità dei Monti, the Persian and the Frenchman were often to be seen praying side by side. When the Angelus began to ring Zitli was back at the Capuchin friary—Benedict Labre was once more in the hospice.

Lanterns swung before and behind carriages as the social world began to wake up to life. It was the hour when *conversaziones* were held in the Roman palazzos.

The twelve poor inmates of the hospice were gathered together for the evening. They would pass the time telling stories of witches burned, devils cast out, shepherdesses becoming queens. And in their own way they also discussed public affairs. One evening, one of them was ranting against "the enemies of the Church" so

loudly that he broke in on the prayers of the French
beggar Benedict, whose self-denial never let him huddle
round the fire with the rest when the winter winds
whistled in round the ill-fitting doors, and who always
chose the worst mattress that no one else wanted. "The
enemies of the Church!" cried the zealot. These beggars
knew that the power which so complacently gave them
their bread and butter was being attacked, and they
bristled up like faithful dogs whose master was in danger.
Pius VI's encyclicals denounced the impiety seeping in
everywhere, "in the large public schools, in the houses of
the great, in the courts of kings, and even in the sanctuary". These wretches who imposed their faith rather
like a boxer dealing a hard punch, chorused loudly:
"Excommunications are what is needed! The enemies of
the Church must be excommunicated!" Benedict, to
whom this meant abandoning them utterly to the darkness, made a half gesture of supplication, of mediation
between these nameless culprits and the justice of the
ignorant, that most inexorable justice of all. A saint never
breaks the bent branch—nor snuffs out the candle wick
that is still smoking.

"Curse the devil that started these evils in the Church!"
pursued the zealot. Benedict quietly opened his Bible
and tried to explain to his companions that we have no
right to curse any being, even the devil, who is God's
creature and entirely in God's hands, and who, by receiving God's punishment, is part of the order of things.
Benedict found the text he wanted in the Epistle of Saint
Jude, and he read aloud the mysterious words: "When
Michael the Archangel disputing with the devil, con-
tended about the body of Moses, he durst not bring

against him the judgment of railing speech, but said: The Lord command thee".

Usually, when Benedict thought the others were offending against charity, he would cry, "Think of Our Lord's passion!" or, pointing skywards, "Look at the stars".

Could Joseph II be included among "the enemies of the Church"? He had declared war to the death upon the contemplative orders and had no qualms about suppressing one or other of them outright wherever he had the power. Joseph wanted the accumulated wealth of the monks more than their prayers. It was to settle Church matters with the Emperor of Austria that Pius VI set out for Vienna in 1782. He left Rome on February 17. Benedict's poor companions followed the train of coaches and barouches; their cries of loyalty were lost in an immense acclamation when, by the Porta del Popolo, Pius VI dismissed the noble guard, and exchanged his pontifical robes for travelling dress. All the beggars knelt to receive the apostolic blessing. Benedict, that day, had gone to visit a sick friend near the Colosseum. His hospice-companions that evening, bubbling over like children at the excitements of the day, asked him whether he had also been there to see the Holy Father go by. "What is the good of seeing him?" he answered, roused, it seemed, from a melancholy meditation, "What is the good of seeing him? We must pray for him". They always noticed how sad Benedict grew when there was talk of Pius VI, and, scandalised, his companions muttered, "He says it does no good to see the Pope!" What about the blessings? And the indulgences? Was this foreigner a heretic too?

While the plague ravaged Dalmatia, and earthquakes

shook Sicily and Calabria, these poor creatures were congratulating themselves on being in Rome, the holy city.
They luxuriated in their sense of security. But Benedict
warned them against such credulous and superstitious
confidence. "These ordeals may spread to Rome", he
would say. He was perhaps foreseeing cataclysms of an
order other than earthquakes. In a town where the leaders
of thought were occupied with the musical comedies of
Metastasio and the claims of rival actresses to get the
crown of honour at the capitol, Benedict went to see his
confessor Father Marconi to describe a dream persist-
ently troubling him: was it some mirage sent by the devil?
"I see a huge fire driving across my country. . . ." The
blaze was consuming abbeys where he had stayed; the
Blessed Sacrament was being profaned on the altars;
God's priests were being persecuted. Benedict was de-
scribing the French Revolution.[1] Marconi knew that his
penitent was not given to hallucinations, nor was he
specially excitable. He reassured him, though he was
himself quite disturbed. After all, mankind was in the
arms of God, and however great his anguish Benedict
never lost the sort of peasant wisdom which knows that
God tempers the wind to the shorn lamb. But the destroying fire in his vision drove him to even greater
mortifications. He was never the prophet spreading terror.
"He always came like an angel of peace", was the universal witness to his life.

Benedict used to teach his companions at the hospice
to abandon themselves to Providence; "God only gives

---

[1] Benedict told the same things he had told Father Marconi to a nun
in Verona.

us trials because He loves us, and we please Him by abandoning ourselves to His fatherly care", he would say, and as he spoke he seemed bathed in light. But when the supernatural rays faded away the inmates of the little hospice were still the same embittered men they always had been. There were unpleasant moments. There was low sarcastic laughter. "The holy Frenchman" was their favourite subject for bullying. One humourist, a certain Saturnino, much dreaded, for there was nothing he dared not say, would open the attack: "Well, Benedict, are we going to see you going up to heaven again?" The miraculous levitations that astonished them also served for their most vulgar jokes. Now Benedict trusted his ecstasies as little as his visions of the future. Whatever might as easily have come from the devil as from God was suspect. Such mockery as this only served to establish him more firmly in his fear and humility. "When are you going to fly away, Benedict?" asked another enemy, a man they nicknamed "the priest" because of the ecclesi-astical cut of his clothes. And one weak-minded old fellow, whose obscenity offended Benedict's purity, also sniggered from his corner: "When'll we see you taking off again?"

Once, there was a census, and Benedict was obliged to state particulars about himself before his companions which he would rather have kept secret. He told his name, his parents' status, his birthplace, Amettes, in the diocese of Boulogne, France.

"France!" cried one of his fellow-boarders, "Bologna, France! Did you hear that?" So they had caught this preacher of truth in the very act of lying! "Bologna is in

Italy you know", agreed a deceptively friendly voice, "There is no Bologna in France".

"Liar! Hypocrite! *Santocchio! Gabbamondo!*" And on that hateful evening, they found the most cruel insult of all: "*Figlio di camminante!*" cried one. Against his will, because he could do no other, Benedict had revealed his parentage and his province. But so totally had he given himself over to the luck of the highroad, that he was to belong to the highroad forever. The family of respectable farmers, the home he loved, were his no more. They did not even believe these things existed—or at least they pretended not to. They were lumping him together with the gypsies, with all the world's homeless wanderers. "Tramp! Son of a tramp! *Figlio di camminante!*" shouted his hospice companions.

"Bologna isn't in France", repeated the geography master, "I've travelled all over France, and I never found any Bologna there!"

"If you know France", retorted Benedict, "you must know Boulogne—Boulogne-sur-Mer".

He stopped himself on the threshold of getting impatient. One evening, "while discussing the wars of the day", as the Beatification Process tells us, one man broke out into the most offensive remarks about France. Benedict was roused, and it was only with the greatest difficulty that he restrained his anger. Tramp, *figlio di camminante* maybe, but he still had a country.

Benedict had taken all the misery of the poor upon himself, but for a long time he could not sacrifice his solitude: he was now making his holocaust perfect by adding to his other trials the trial of these men's company.

The Way of the Cross at the Colosseum

He wept over the coarseness of his companions, without knowing that, in the end, he would sanctify them all. All—even the most unpromising, even the coarsest—found themselves imperceptibly and in spite of heavy backslidings, ascending willy nilly with him.

By the end of a year, the inmates of the hospice were up in the middle of the night to sing the Te Deum; Benedict's voice, which could be heard among the rest, shook with more than ordinary thankfulness. But often, during night prayers, when time came for the invocation "Praised be the most holy Sacrament of the altar forever", Benedict's lips simply refused to move. Rigid as a corpse, he contemplated the Love that expressed Itself in the breaking of bread. While the rest galloped noisily through the final Our Fathers, the warden of the hospice glanced uneasily at the one who remained silent: intensity of faith was taken for doubt. He warned the director Father Mancini, who murmured, "I really must have a word with the parish priest". And Father Mancini and the parish priest of San Martino dei Monti, a Carmelite,[1] discussed at great length the beggar who was the edification of the neighbourhood. A Jansenist? Surely not! And yet, why should he stiffen up like that during the adoration of the Blessed Sacrament?

"We might perhaps bring him before the Holy Office for his own good", was the charitable conclusion of their priestly conversation.

"Do not believe that the Holy Office is really as bad as it seems", wrote the Président de Brosses. But neither the threat of the Holy Office, nor even that of a short

---

[1] Father Moschini, later one of the adversaries of the Beatification.

imprisonment for his own good, worried Benedict; and in fact, the plan was never carried out. The priest of San Martino dei Monti was content to reproach Benedict for his strange behaviour. Why did he not have the joy—even once a year—of seeing him at Communion in his church, the parish of the hospice? But the priest was not so much imposing a duty as asking a favour. He did not speak *in the name of obedience*. In spite of everything, he had too good an opinion of Benedict to do that. Benedict hung his head and said, "I am a sinful man".

After his death, it was proved by comparing authentic witnesses that he had always received Communion at the earliest Masses, in churches where he was least known. Jansenist ideas were being severely denounced in Italy at that time. And Alphonsus Liguori, their chief opponent, recommended weekly Communion as the best cure. In the year of his death, Benedict took up this practice. He sided against the Jansenists, but appearances were against him. He was certainly not a model parishioner. But after all, he was a tramp—he could never think of himself as belonging to any parish except Amettes in the diocese of Boulogne. The fire of God takes hold of the saints. But it never entirely burns away the old man; it could not destroy the proud, sensitive, reserved nature of Benedict Labre. This son of the soil held fast to his soul as he would have held fast to his land unless God had ordered him to let it go. The priest of San Martino pushed clumsily on: "Shall I see you at Communion in my parish? . . . Let me see your latest Communion certificate. . . . It would give me great joy to give you Communion on the feast that is coming!" Benedict fumbled in his wallet for the certificate: he had of course lost it.

The Way of the Cross at the Colosseum

The accusation of Jansenism stung him—all the more reason for not clearing himself. He shuffled off, saying, "Yes . . . Yes . . . I'll see about it . . . *Bene, bene . . . vedremo. . . .*" The words he most liked borrowing from Italian were those expressing prudence and procrastination, the words peasants use to elude the unwelcome curiosity of strangers

Benedict would only reveal what was in his soul to his confessors. There were three in Rome whose names are known to us: one Frenchman, Père Tisson, father penitentiary of Saint John Lateran, and two Italians, Fathers Gabrini and Marconi. Marconi, in particular, was very much on his guard against the French heresies—"rigid opinions", he said, "demanding a purity of conscience and of love quite beyond a mere man".[1] He also feared that Benedict might have a taint of Jansenism. But he asked him some questions about grace, and the clear and humble answers he got set his mind at rest.

There was no heresy in Benedict; but there was one thing that gave rise to suspicion: that trembling before the Host, that fear which had filled him in childhood and did not fully leave him until the last weeks before his death: "I am a sinful man", he groaned, "I am not worthy to receive the Bread of Angels". He received Communion because his confessors told him to. His obedience saved him. He came out most strongly against Jansenist religious customs. "It is better", said he, "to go to Communion out of obedience than to stay away out of humility".

And yet, when he left Rome at the end of the cold weather to go to Loreto, the director of the hospice was

[1] Statement of the witness Father Marconi.

sadly reproachful of his going. Was not this journey a trick to dodge making his Easter duty? And the Carmelite priest of San Martino dei Monti perused the notebook where he had listed his faithful parishioners who practised their religion, his register of souls. The inmates of the hospices were all listed except one—the one who was later to be canonised.

Chapter Seven

The Road to Loreto

SOUTH of Ancona, the countryside along the Adriatic changes. Small towns crown the hills—Osimo, Castel-filardo. And on one small hill between the Apennines and the sea, a light-coloured cupola stands out, so exquisite, that even in this land of pleasing cupolas, it strikes the eye and stays in the mind. The peasant women of Romagna and Umbria, talking along in groups praying aloud as they go, will sing as it comes into view:

Evviva Maria . . .
Maria Evviva . . .

They are saluting Loreto, which, with Saint James at Compostella, was one of the major pilgrimages of Christendom. At the beginning of the fourteenth century a marvellous rumour spread—for the world then did not find the idea of miracles offensive. To a laurel wood in the region of Recanati an oriental house had been transported, it was said, by angels, Our Lady's Nazareth home, the Holy House; this cradle of Christianity had been given to the West. Crowds came to see. Great names stand out from those crowds, over the course of years. Were they all simple, uneducated souls? They included men called Montaigne, Galileo, Descartes. Tasso, too poor to give Our Lady an ex-voto, offered her instead a *Canzone*. It was other pilgrims than these that showed Benedict the way, and filled him with their spirit. Jean-Jacques Olier, the founder of Saint Sulpice, climbed the hill of Loreto in the heat of summer, wearing thick woollen clothes to do penance. At the dawn of the eighteenth century the missionary, Grignon de Montfort, with his Bible and his breviary in his bag, made his way to the famous shrine, begging his bread, to return and stir the whole of the Vendée by his sermons and his hymns. Between 1770 and 1782, Benedict made the pilgrimage to Loreto eleven times. He usually came from Rome at about Easter.

The first impression one gets of Loreto is rather warlike: there are ramparts built to protect the unarmed settlement of priests and merchants against the onslaughts of pirates; they stand high and defiant like a fortress. And then one comes suddenly upon all the pomp of the Renaissance: porticoes, balustrades, an ever-flowing fountain, and, in front of the church, a very ornate statue of Pope Sixtus V. The austerity of the Middle Ages had vanished. In the square paved with flagstones there is a richness of decoration, an entirely Italian magnificence where space is no object. Inside the shrine is a flowing murmur of prayer, the slow stream of a whole tradition. A gorgeous monument rises from behind the altar— Corinthian columns, garlands, the whiteness of the bas-reliefs with their figures of sybils and of prophets. Here and there one's foot finds a sort of channel hollowed into the floor: century by century, the pilgrims of Loreto have worn these furrows by circling round the chapels on their knees. It is a place where wealth is the frame for poverty; palazzos contain the austere cells of nuns, and this great marble case contains the barest room of all, the *Santa Casa,* the Holy House of Nazareth. By the light of votive lamps you can read the words that explain the existence of the community here, the presence of the crowds: "Here it is that the Word was made flesh".

In the eighteenth century, the contrast between grandeur and rags was even more striking than it is today. The ex-votos of kings shone in the sanctuary with their fire of gold and diamonds, while an underfed population adhered like a leprosy to the sides of the hill. Strangers had simply to stop their ears to avoid being deafened by the shouts of the beggars, and throwing a few *bajoccos* from their carriage windows, would note in the diaries of their travels the disgust they felt: "As one approaches Loreto, and indeed, throughout that district, wrote Jérome de Lalande, "one is overwhelmed by beggars who ask for alms and kiss the ground in a way that would distress anyone".[1]

Benedict had, according to his destiny, to sink himself among these dregs in order to purify them; he took their misery so utterly upon himself that he was lost among them. He hurried to the Santa Casa, read the words, "Here it is that the Word was made flesh", and was seized with a trembling adoration. He never doubted for an instant that this was the very room where, by the power of the Holy Ghost, Our Lady had conceived Christ our Redeemer. As a scholar would abstract himself from

[1] *Voyage d'un Français en Italie,* 1765–1766.

the outer world by a methodical effort, so Benedict made a kind of spiral descent to the depths of his prayer. He succeeded in shutting out the too operatic music; he came at once to the very heart of his faith. All he saw was a little oriental house where an Archangel once appeared. And slowly, this over-concrete image too went, and only the thought of the Incarnation remained.

When time came to close the Santa Casa for the night, the Corsican soldiers who stood guard in front of the little chapel had to send him out. He went obediently, but he did not go far. He lay down with his bag for a pillow, in front of one of the bronze doors. Bas-reliefs portrayed the symbols of eternal mediation: Jacob's ladder, the brazen serpent, the Ark of the Covenant, Esther's petitioning. Benedict, with all his scruples, slept alongside them, lying happy in the hope of his salvation. One morning, before the Angelus had rung, a young priest noticed him. Valeri was his name; he had only just been ordained and was carrying out the duties of sacristan. The sight of this human wreck went to his heart. He spoke kindly to him, with that protective pity one feels for homeless emigrants; he offered to write to his family, to arrange for him to be sent home. "But", related Father Valeri, "this poor man did not want to tell me anything about his family, or where he came from". However, Benedict did mention Rome as the central point of his pilgrimages. Valeri asked him for his address there. The beggar's face lit up. The idea of having an address, like a respectable citizen, and knowing that he would not be spending any given night in gaol, clearly amused him. "Here and there", he answered, smiling. "Sometimes here, sometimes there". The priest pointed out that the icy draught coming from the bell-tower was enough to kill him, and that there were charitable Christians in the neighbourhood who would certainly give him lodging. "A poor man", declared Benedict, "must be satisfied with what he finds: the ground is quite good enough". The priest persisted: he would like to find him somewhere to stay; and in the end the pilgrim went with him. They went out together by the Marine gate, and set off downwards towards the Adriatic. "What would people say", Benedict wondered aloud, "if they saw a priest like you going about with a poor wretch like me!" He held the priesthood in high honour, and was always highly conscious of his own baseness. Because it was a priest who told him to, he spent the night in some peasant's house; but this meant going some distance from the basilica, and he hated losing so much time, and missing his icy slumbers on the flagstones by the porch. He sometimes made his way up into the mountains to venerate the miraculous crucifix of Sirolo.

On his fifth pilgrimage, Benedict made friends with the father penitentiary in charge of French pilgrims, Père Temple.[1] He was a Friar Minor, originally from Turin, and was held to be a very learned theologian. He lamented that the ages of pilgrimage were gone forever. The pilgrims he had to deal with now were hypocrites with more stolen coins than medals in their pockets, men who found it pleasanter to pass as contemplatives than to work, or criminals with forged passports who had slipped through the fingers of the police. He had seen too much of man's mediocrity, of the depths of trickery he could

---

[1] On earlier pilgrimages, Benedict's confessor had been a Jesuit, Father Bodetty.

resort to, and he was becoming embittered. He could be heard in the sacristy venting his impatience with the unholy crew. One day, Benedict appeared, following upon the heels of two complete swindlers, and Père Temple, who was by nature rigid and untrusting, at once took him for a third. The beggar announced that he would like to place himself under Père Temple's direction. The priest put a few questions to him, and his answers showed a degree of resignation and abandonment that quite bewildered the practical man. What did he live on? asked the priest. Benedict listed his means of subsistence: the soup distributed at convents and monasteries, the refuse of the markets, things still quite edible that people threw out as rubbish, and, when all else failed, wild fruit and roots. If there was something poetic in this gradual descent from the soup ladled out by the generosity of a lay brother to the thirst-quenching bush sloe, it was lost on Père Temple. He did not like eccentrics. Rather sharply he asked to see the poor man's latest certificates of confession and Communion. It was quite usual to ask this of pilgrims. There were charitable institutions specially for them: it must at least be shown that they practised their religion. Benedict made no answer, produced no certificate. Père Temple, whose patience soon wore thin, labelled him *Huguenot.* More French pilgrims had come in; they stared, with the foolish gaze of those to whom scandal comes easily, at this offender, this pariah, this bad Catholic. It was because he felt himself being watched that Benedict stood so silent—the accused judging himself guilty. He went out, and came back to see Père Temple when he was alone; he pulled the papers in question out of his wallet—they were in perfect order.

The Road to Loreto

Père Temple was amazed. Why had he let himself be called a Huguenot like that, without a word? "Well, all those French people were there", he answered, "all those French people were standing round".

Strange modesty that would hinder a beggar from mentioning what sacraments he had received in public! For many of the faithful at that date—and even for some of the clergy—they were simply formalities one went through so as not to cut oneself off from a whole ancient and venerable way of life. It is easy enough to talk about rites and formulas, but not so easy to talk of a love that is consuming the whole soul. Benedict hated men to see him as someone reborn in sanctifying grace, raised to the level of heaven. Their insults were far better suited to his humiliation. Père Temple continued to frown; he had intended to write Benedict off in the register with the uncompromising words: "Suspected of heresy and hypocrisy". But under his hand the wording changed to: "Suspected of immense contempt for himself". He looked at the pilgrim and knew that his impulse had been right. Men usually shrink from insults, but saints delight in them. Saints! In a flash Père Temple saw this poor man as a victim among the rubbish.

During the days that followed, priest and pilgrim had long talks in the Penitentiary Chapel.

The poor man protected his spiritual life from any intrusion, but by questioning him *in the name of obedience,* Père Temple managed to extract from him his soul. Benedict told him the intentions he prayed for. There were many—his prayer covered almost all mankind—like small children who lump them together in immense groups in their Night Prayers. For all these

great groups—infidels, sinners, heretics, schismatics—
Benedict was a living sacrifice. He told of his sufferings,
how sometimes his soul itself, in that body which was
more like a dead body, seemed to die, when God hid
Himself. "When that happens", said Benedict, "I unite
my loneliness with the loneliness of Christ in the Garden
of Olives". Benedict's was often the suffering prayer of
Job. The familiarity of faith lessened his agony somewhat.
"O my Beloved", he would pray, when the darkness
lifted, "I thought of Thee during this night in which
Thou didst cause me such anguish, in which Thou madest
me to shed such tears. I supposed that my thanklessness
had driven Thee to do the bidding of Thy justice and
remove Thyself from me. I sighed, I ran to find you, and
I found only darkness. Never doubt, my Saviour, that I
am all Thine, for the first impulse of my heart is to
convince me that Thou still lovest me this day, and that
Thou art not as far from me as my sins deserve. But
when, Lord, Thou dost go far from me, I will still hope
in Thee!"

Year by year his joys came more and more to outweigh
his sorrows. In youth Benedict had been haunted by the
vision of a universe heavy with guilt; a new vision was
gradually taking its place: that of a world reborn in the
blood of Christ. Benedict wept with joy to think of the
Redemption. He who had once found it so painful to
deprive himself of ripe September fruits was now hearing
the trees and grass singing the Magnificat. By his asceticism he had preserved nature's purity; he had set it apart
from our sensualities and lusts. Every landscape now
reflected God, and he could gaze freely at it. If he heard
the howling of demons in men's blasphemies, every

The Road to Loreto

flower he saw recalled to him the splendour of the Trinity. "God's omnipotence, greatness, and magnificence", Père Temple was to say later, "the poor man was so exalted when he talked of these divine attributes that I felt I was listening to a prophet". His chief devotion was the Trinity, the mystery furthest removed from all human concerns. This beggar went straight to God's very Godhead; he fed upon the inaccessible; he prayed more to archangels than to saints, and he felt strongly how much man needed the whole angelic order. Benedict spoke of the Trinity in terms so profound, so perfectly in tune with theology, that he reminded Père Temple of Saint Teresa. No one but she had spoken of the Trinity with that kind of emphasis. "Have you read Saint Teresa?", he asked. Benedict stammered out, "I'm not an educated man, Father", in the same evasive way in which he answered those who asked him whether he knew much Latin. He might perhaps have read one or other of Saint Teresa's works. But at the heart of all his confidences, which sometimes bordered on ecstasy, there was a barrier, a sort of reserve, one might almost say of peasant cunning. He retired into his soul's private oratory.

Benedict Labre had sought out Père Temple to ask him one particular point. The more he wandered, the more he longed for monastic stability. "The harshest order, with the strictest observance": that was what he had always longed for, and he longed for it still. He was now past thirty, and he felt that his perseverance was coming towards its end and reward. He told Père Temple of his wish to join the Camaldolese. We might be tempted to call it his anxiety, or his homesickness, but no word of that kind can convey the exact notion. Benedict was above all patient and sorrowing.

In France, the Commission des Réguliers had announced the suppression of the Camaldolese. Their report described them as of edifying piety, but "unable to keep themselves alive or enrol new members"[1]. By 1769 there were only eighteen of them left; they disbanded without protest. They were an old order, dating from the same time as the Servites and the Celestines. However, Benedict had come to know the Camaldolese not in his own country, but in Italy, where they were flourishing. Their hermitages nestled against mountainsides, and the sharp outline of a bell-tower would mark their high place of expiation. Long ago, the founder of the Camaldolese, Saint Romuald, had set about introducing the asceticism of the East into the West. His rule for his followers had to be mitigated as time went on, but it still reflected its early austerity, and it was the closest thing Benedict could find to Abbot de Rancé's Trappists. As he venerated Saint Romuald's tomb at Fabriano, he knew that in the nearby Apennines there was a settlement of their little huts amid the snows of Mount Catria. From Loreto, the pilgrim could see Mount Conaro with its great bare mass commanding the Adriatic; there too, these religious practised their austerities, wearing their white, Trappist-like robes. It was the Mount Conaro hermitage that Benedict fixed upon—Benedict the anachronism, seeking admission to orders whose very existence seemed pointless to the age he lived in. To join the Mount Conaro Camaldolese! Benedict told Père Temple how ardently he wanted this. The priest considered; then, with a sudden inspiration,

[1] S. Lemaire, *La Commission des Réguliers* (Paris, 1926), p. 152.

and as if by some authority not his own, he declared: "No, my son; that is not God's plan for you". Benedict Labre submitted. From then on, having placed his longing to be a monk entirely in the hands of God, he moved deeper and deeper into the place of peace.

Père Temple wanted to keep some record of his talks with this extraordinary pilgrim to Our Lady. Each evening he made brief notes in Latin, the broken phrases one uses to crystallise a strong emotion at once, leaving the arrangement of the ideas till later. After Benedict's death, when his cause of beatification was introduced, Père Temple's notes were to be a most precious document. One day Benedict chanced to hear that this priest who had handled him so roughly not only did not despise him, but actually thought highly of him. This so upset him, that from that moment whenever he saw Père Temple he avoided him.

There was a woman from the neighbourhood, Barbara Sori, who used to watch the beggar praying in the holy house of Loreto. She, too, came to the conclusion that he was a saint, but in a quite different way from Père Temple. She was one of those women who kept a stall of not very popular little statues and medals, and she also ran a boarding house on mercenary enough lines, though she was pious all the same. Her type could be seen in the Santa Casa every day, winding a rosary around the hands of a bambino too small to say it with them. Barbara Sori did not believe there was an infinite distance between heaven and earth, but only the finest of screens; she thanked God for the privilege of living near the Holy House of Loreto. But this grace did not exempt her from trials. Several of her children had died in infancy, and Barbara was invoking Our Lady for another that was soon to be born. At the back of the shop, her husband, Gaudentio, was counting his money dolefully in spite of his joyful name. He owed his creditors four hundred scudi. It was a moment of poverty, weariness and apprehension, the moment for Benedict Labre to come on the scene. The woman had always given Benedict the widest berth possible, but not from shocked horror: it was only natural for pilgrims to be dirty, poor things, *poverini,* tramping over mountains, sleeping on the ground. But there was a glow from heaven that seemed to shine from his abjectness. Barbara Sori was suddenly amazed to find that this loathsome poor creature reminded her of the beautiful face of Christ she had seen pictures of. *Come to me, all ye that labour.* . . .

The simple Italians who had their own way of seeing Benedict's holiness admitted that at first sight they were torn between an almost unconquerable disgust and a fear bordering on shame. *Ribrezzo* . . . *Rispetto.* Childlike, they described the struggle between the two. In the end, veneration drove out repugnance, and in the triumph of this inexplicable respect, these unlearned, simple people would try to attract the pilgrim's notice by giving him an alms, asking his help. The boldest among them invited him to a meal, or even begged him to stay with them. His position at the bottom of the social ladder was a cover for the dizzy ascent of his soul; he had risen to being despised. And that was what the woman with the boarding house sensed. "Don't judge by appearances": how easily that is said. Yet it is only truly understood by those who value the spiritual—like this poor soul, with her rosary-selling and her simple, homely piety. If only she could take the pilgrim into her house! In a burst of charity she longed for such a privilege, not stopping to think that his lice might frighten off her small clientèle. What did that matter if he could charm away death and disaster? Barbara Sori found that her husband wanted him to come as much as she did. That same evening they sent the maid, Maria Diamante, along to the Basilica to invite him. Benedict agreed: "I will accept this charity". Maria brought him back, muttering to herself, "I'd like to throw him and his rags into the river". We do not know for certain whether Benedict was willing to undergo this bath. But we do know that Barbara Sori and her maid managed to force upon him entirely clean clothes, and the new linen of his shirt threw him into the same sort of raptures as the food that held his body together, the delight of utter detachment. He still grumbled as he admired and thanked; he begged to be allowed to keep his rags. Priests saw that he was a mystic; those who knew him talked far more about the shoes he thought tattered enough to accept, the coat he refused because it was made of such good wool, the black hood he could hardly take off quickly enough, thinking it might make people take him for a cleric and thus bring ridicule on the priesthood.

As he prepared to set off back across the mountains, Barbara Sori was knitting him stockings. Her intuition told her the unfailing formula to use on this monk-in-spirit—she ordered Benedict "in the name of obedience" to accept her gifts. Gaudentio, her husband, confided his money troubles to their guest, and his wife scolded him for it;—she ascertained that Benedict had contrived to

put a few farthings in the poor-box;—but she asked him
to pray that all would go well with the approaching birth
of her child. With his usual perfect politeness, he
answered: "Gratitude demands that I pray for my benefactors". When she bemoaned the sorrows of life, Benedict did not contradict her, as might some jovial, well-fed
priest. The great prayers of the liturgy he called to mind
distributed none of that sort of cheap optimism: *ad te
suspiramus, gementes et flentes in hac lacrimarum valle.*
"The world is a vale of tears", said Benedict, "and we
shall only be consoled the other side of the tomb. . . . We
must despise ourselves and be humiliated, we must pray
at the foot of the cross, we must trust ourselves utterly to
God's goodness, and wait with hope and resignation for
whatever life may bring . . ." Sorrow melted away in utter
serenity. All his courage, all his energy went into that
acceptance, that utterly simple doctrine which would make
a man a saint. But though he was so holy, Barbara Sori
feared sometimes for the stranger's salvation. She had
never seen him receiving Communion. Did he make his
Easter duties? Here, as in Rome, Benedict, who was
always under some suspicion of heresy, found himself
open to the pestering of busybodies, questions he disliked
answering, and unconscious spying which went by the
name of zeal. The most uneducated knew something of
Jansenism. "Knowing that Benedict was French", reports
Barbara Sori in the Beatification Process, "I was at once
afraid that he might be the sort that lives outwardly as a
good Catholic and a good Christian, but is not really a
Catholic at all". This vague mistrust attached to him
simply as a Frenchman. And Barbara Sori, while he was
in the basilica praying, thought herself quite justified—

for must we not fight heresy whenever we find it?—in searching her guest's wallet, where she found proof that this holy man was a practising Catholic.

You can still see the room where Benedict slept in the Soris' house, dark and uncomfortable, as he wished it: a corner of the cellar with a plank and mattress laid on trestles. The silence of the night was broken by his voice praying: "O God, do Thou strengthen my faith, increase my hope. Thou art my share in the land of the living . . . Jesus, Son of David, have mercy on me . . ." Benedict begged of God the virtues that only His presence could impart to men. When he announced his departure, his host offered him a few pence, but Benedict refused in his usual words: "The poor don't carry money on their journeys. . . ." That was one of the maxims he used to tell over to himself as he went, one of the terrifying laws he had made for his misery: "The poor have scraps of bread, not whole loaves . . . The poor should not be well dressed . . . The poor must mortify themselves and overcome their flesh just like everyone else. . . ." He went off, so weak, so utterly unprovided, that Gaudentio and Barbara Sori were quite worried. But the next year, as the organ began again to groan out the approaching death of Our Lord, Benedict Labre, wallet on shoulder, reappeared in the doorway of the little inn.

In 1782, Benedict set off from Rome to Loreto for the last time. The generous butcher Zaccarelli, from the Monti district, seeing the pilgrim going along bareheaded, offered him an old hat of his. Benedict was delighted as he put it on: "I look like a lord in this"—*paro un milordo*. He was always laughing at himself, and his good humour increased towards his death. Zaccarelli's wife wanted to give him the money to have a Mass said at the Santa Casa. But Benedict would not take it: "Mass is the same, here or there". Pilgrim that he was, he would have no superstitious devotion to pilgrimages. And when Signora Zaccarelli exclaimed, "How lucky you are to visit those holy places!" Benedict would answer rather sharply, "How lucky are they who do God's will!" He read in his *Imitation*: "There are few who become saints by making many pilgrimages", and Benedict always thought with the *Imitation*. He knew that obeying grace was the only pledge of salvation, and that it was not crossing the Apennines that mattered.

The journey of 1782 was longer and harder than the previous ones. How dangerous it was we can judge from this sentence from an old Italian guide: "Between the Case Nuove and Seravalle, is the Colfiorito, quite a dangerous pass during the winter because of the terrific eddies of snow, what they call the *bufa,* especially during or just after a snowfall[1]." Such was the road Benedict took as he set off from Foligno to Tolentino that early Eastertide, with winter still clinging to the mountains. Alone, more completely alone with God than ever, amid the roaring of the torrents he might have disappeared as finally as a pebble rolling down a gorge. At last he got to the fortified township of Tolentino which brings to an end the crossing of the Apennines. He venerated the town's patron saint in his richly adorned chapel, and then went into a small shop. The proprietress at once recognised him as the man who had given her a vial of that *manna* from the tomb of St. Nicholas at Bari, which

[1] Tiroli: *Le véritable Guide des Voyageurs en Italie* (1775).

cured all ills. She asked the pilgrim whether he had any more of the miraculous stuff. Benedict had none, but he drew from his wallet a medal and some small crucifixes. The superstitious woman had no notion that this was a saint offering her future relics, and these worthless little pious objects seemed to her of no importance compared with the famous *manna* of Bari, St. Nicholas' *manna*. "Some other time . . . some other time", she mumbled, to get rid of the pilgrim and his useless generosity. "But", said he, "I may never come this way again!" and his face lit up with unspoken hope. He seemed like an exile with the reason and the length of his banishment known only to himself. And it was then that the pilgrim said the extraordinary thing. The child of peasants, whose whole life is a saving, a hoarding and a handing on, Benedict was destroying all trace of his personality. He took care never to give his name—he scarcely ever told anyone except priests. He usually told people simply that he was their brother in Christ: "I am a Christian . . . I am a Christian"; and he rather implied: And now please leave me in peace. But at Tolentino, he gave his name of his own accord, and quite insistently. Deep in a seemingly endless abyss, he had felt the anguish of the senses that comes before death. Was that why he broke his long silence, his long rule of self-abasement, to impress himself on the memory of this stranger? "If I should happen to die in Rome", he said to the proprietress of the shop, "and you shouldn't happen to hear of it, I'd like you to know that my name is Labre . . . *Labre*". He reiterated the mournful word, with its overtones of hunger, thirst, raggedness.

He set off once more: he had ten leagues to go to

Loreto. But at Monte Lupone, heavy rain held him up. Two brothers, Antonio and Felix Palotto, lived near a monastery and ran its farm. They found the poor creature lying under their steps, pale and soaking. They practised the works of mercy towards Our Lady's pilgrims; Benedict was revived with hot herb and vegetable soup, and when night came, the peasants made a place for him in the cattle shed. Because he was a stranger, they bolted the doors.

The conversations the brothers had with their neighbours in the evenings were very curious at that time.

"It *is* annoying", said one, "that you can't see the stars in this filthy weather! When they are up close to the moon, the high numbers always win in the lottery".

"If we were in Rome", said another voice, "we could go up the Ara Coeli steps saying the Hail Mary and the De Profundis, and praying to the Three Wise Men as well".

"If we were in Rome", responded the first voice with a hint of fear in it, "we could make the novena to executed criminals".

A shudder ran through the group clustered in the darkness. Breath came gaspingly.

"Yes, I know that novena to the executed", said one old woman. "You've got to go at night along the exact way the poor wretches were taken to their death, and then you go to the Church of the Beheading of St. John where they bury them if they've received the sacraments. You kneel down and say the Kyrie Eleison, and the souls of the ones who have expiated their crimes whisper the right numbers to you. It's a sure way, but you sometimes die of fright, because they sometimes appear, all white in the darkness, with no heads, or with their heads in their hands".

There was some chattering of teeth, and a long silence.

"You're all right if you have a lucky charm", said a voice trying to be calm. "A shirt worn by one of the criminals is enough".

"There are the pilgrims and beggars that God enlightens and brings to us", reminded one pious voice, rather reprovingly. "And there are the saints. Don't forget the saints".

A murmur of approval echoed through the group:

"Yes, the saints: St. Alexis. . . ."

"Saint Pantaleone is better. . . ."

"Oh no, Saint Alexis. . . ."

The group split into two factions, one for Saint Alexis, one for Saint Pantaleone.

"The novena to Saint Alexis works quite differently", said one party. "All you have to do is sleep under the steps of your own house like he used to. Then you go out at midnight, and the most ordinary country noises, an owl, or a donkey braying, or a dog barking—anything might give you the right number".

"The novena to Saint Pantaleone is better", said the others. "At midnight—and it is essential that you should be in a room where you have slept by yourself—you must wake up shouting: 'Long live St. Pantaleone! Give us the right number!' And if you have left paper and ink on the table, the saint writes the number down for you".

"That's true", said the tremulous voice with relish for the terror it produced. "But sometimes the saint himself appears in the room. One woman shook so much with

fright that she died of it. The next day her husband found
the winning numbers written in shining figures!"

They were peasants who would be placidly digging or
pulling off mulberry leaves the next day as usual, who
were saying these wild things. One lucky chance might
transform their cottages into the sort of mansions lords
lived in: *Il lotto,* the lottery—it was the one miracle in
their humdrum lives, the promise that gleamed on the
horizon, all the more fascinating because it was never
realised. The lottery was soon to be drawn in Rome, in
the Palace of Monte Citorio, according to the time-
honoured custom, before a crowd who had in the pre-
ceding week tried every sort of queer omen and mangled
devotion. Heaven knew how many old women would
have gone up the long Ara Coeli steps on their knees.
The novena to executed criminals was a widespread practice, and any number of credulous souls would have
spent the night wandering about the Church of St. John's
Beheading. They even came to the asylums and most
earnestly asked advice of the lunatics. The essential
features of popular customs always persist. And even
today it is quite easy to find trace of these curiosities. But
in sleepy, eighteenth-century Italy, the lottery craze—that
factor of decadence—had run riot in a way we can
scarcely credit. Here in this village lost in the Marshes
of Ancona it possessed the souls of two peasants, Antonio
and Felix.

They were on their way to bed when a sound from the
cowshed caught their attention. They made out the words
of Latin psalms, broken by sobbing: *Miserere mei Deus,
secundum magnam misericordiam tuam.* . . . The pilgrim,

whom they had locked in as a potential robber, was be-
seeching God's everlasting love. "He looked a bit of a
saint", recalled one brother. "When I saw him on the
steps he reminded me of St. Alexis". Saint Alexis! The
ascetic they honoured in Rome—the patron of all who
took part in the lottery! This stranger was quite certainly
enlightened by God, he undoubtedly knew the right
number. Rejoicing, the brothers went to bed, and dreamt
of treasures. At dawn, they drew back the bolts of the
cowshed, and with deep deference approached the beggar, who was still praying, his hands crossed on his chest.
And they could only stand motionless, in dumb respect,
unconsciously submitting to the power of a prayer utterly
untouched by any sort of degrading ulterior motive, as
upright as the pillar of fire in the Bible. All that super-
stition usurped from the spiritual was repaid by Benedict
as he prayed. Nervous, beating about the bush, as peasants
will when they open a conversation they find embarras-
sing, Antonio and Felix forced themselves to speak.
"Because of the idea we had formed of this beggar's use-
fulness", they admitted, "we decided to ask him for the
winning number". It had not been an easy thing to do.
With ordinary hermits who shook their money boxes
outside the Church it was simple enough. There was a
certain sly look in their eye, and they found nothing to
object to in a little cupidity—quite the reverse. But this
pilgrim!

"Since you come from Rome", began one, "you have
been there—you can't have missed it—for the drawing of
the lottery".

Il lotto! How Benedict loathed the word. A door-
keeper in Rome, a certain Giuseppe Maittini, had also

once asked him to tell him the winning number. He gave the same account of it as these two peasants: "Because of the high opinion I formed of his sanctity, I thought I might ask him for the number that would win the lottery". Benedict Labre did not understand, or at least pretended not to understand, and the door-keeper withdrew in confusion. So Benedict's holocaust for sinners had come to this! Men who turned ancient sarcophaguses into drinking troughs for their cattle were using his holiness too for mercenary ends. This mockery did not strike him: he suffered simply to think that so many impurities were dragged into prayer. The pilgrim looked at the two brothers: he saw down to the bottom of their hearts, the starting of their corruption, that love of hoarding, that store of avarice gloating over an imaginary gold piece as a lustful desire might embrace a phantom. The two peasants lowered their heads, stirred by a vague remorse. Should they pursue the point? Dared they ask the pilgrim for the winning number? They could not go on. . . .

"*Il lotto!*" exclaimed Benedict, "The lottery! What lottery? The poor have no business thinking about lotteries".

An astounding piece of truth for these villagers. In their simple logic it seemed that the poor were just the people whose business it was. If the pilgrim had said, "The lottery is no affair of the rich" they would have seen some point in it. But the words of the saints come second only to the Gospels for their daring paradox. When Benedict uttered the phrase "the poor", he made its whole meaning sound different. "Show me Lazarus", he demanded one day, when a priest was explaining to him the parable of Dives. The beggar whose wounds the dogs came to lick, and who was welcomed into Abraham's bosom, appeared to Benedict to be a promise of Redemption. When Benedict spoke of poverty it no longer meant the absence of something good: it became a possession itself to be defended. And it was quite independent of gold and silver; it dwelt in the heart. The two peasants of Monte Lupone, small as was their domain, were no longer poor in spirit. And that was why Benedict fixed upon them that sad look they were so long to remember.

As Benedict came to make his last pilgrimage, the dome of Loreto was veiled in fog. The Adriatic, quite hidden, lay dead along an unbroken stretch of sand, more desolate than the sea that washes the shores of Flanders. The afternoon of Maundy Thursday, the Soris heard Benedict's weary salutation: "Praise be to Jesus Christ!" His body was worn down to a minimum: he looked more like a ghost. He said that this journey had been harder than usual, that he had got lost in the mountains. When he had greeted Our Lady, he found that they had prepared a dish of caviare for him—caviare being a very common food in Italy at that time. But Benedict spoke as a beggar might today: "Caviare! That's no dish for the poor!" He would only take bread, uncooked herbs, and water. To Barbara Sori's friendly reproach he would only answer by sighing, "On a night when Christ did nothing but suffer, no, nothing". He did not, as some saints have, bear any stigmata of nails or lance; he relived the Passion in his soul; he was so overcome by this anniversary of suffering that he forgot to eat his bread and herbs. Barbara was afraid, as she watched this man of penance: "How can I be saved", she asked, "when I can't bring myself to suffer?" He was moved by this Italian woman's distress. For a moment the shadows that had been driven out, the scruples that had been beaten back, returned. Benedict thought highly of this woman, and very little of himself. "You are afraid? Then how much more afraid should I be?" It was the evening of Judas' kiss. As the sea mists covered the hill, the shopkeepers of Loreto and the pilgrim were isolated in the intensity of their faith.

Now, several weeks before, Pius VI, on his way to Vienna, had travelled through Ancona, in an impressive exchange of homage and benediction. On March the 2nd he had said Mass in Loreto. This was still the keenest of memories for the Soris. The pilgrim asked them whether the Pope's visit had not brought them more customers than usual. This steady realism was always hand in hand with his contemplation. "How is business going?"— Benedict put to these Italian shopkeepers the question he had heard asked of his own parents, the shopkeepers of their village. At Monte Lupone, he had just upbraided two peasants for looking to the lottery to make them rich. But he took great interest in the bread earned in the sweat of the brow, by crafts, or by the regular give-and-take of the world. He was guided by a lofty sense of vocation. He advised for or against the religious life according to persons and circumstances. He knew that for himself to be destitute was good, but that for most men it was harmful. He never sought imitators. He would show his fellow-men the way to God; and he always directed them away from his own impracticable footpath. Passers-by reproached him for living as a burden on society. They repeated what the Emperor Joseph and his brother, Grand Duke Leopold of Tuscany, had said of contemplatives.

The Road to Loreto

Then Benedict would burrow down in his disgrace. "This is expensive to you", he would sigh, of a mattress, a plateful of soup, a ball of thread. Against the arguments brought to prove how useless he was in the world, he could only set the strong and silent reasoning of his heart, which dictated that he immolate himself for his fellow-men for their spiritual gain, and, by an overflow of charity, for their temporal gain as well. His friends in Loreto needed content and comfort if they were to fulfil their destiny. And for this modest intention Benedict was praying and suffering more than ever. When the innkeeper announced that his debts were all paid off, and the shadow of bankruptcy lifted, Benedict smiled the smile of one whose prayer has been heard. It was late. The pilgrim made a move towards the cellar he slept in. Gaudentio and Barbara Sori warned him that their youngest son was sleeping down there. As parents they were more concerned with devotion than hygiene, and their piety took rather a primitive form: it never occurred to them that it might do their child any harm to be next to so filthy a creature—more than likely they had put him there on purpose. Nervously they asked their guest whether he minded having the cot there. His unshaven face lit up with extraordinary sweetness, as he answered, "No, I shall enjoy it".

Benedict Labre no longer went to see Père Temple, but another confessor at Loreto, Father Almerici. Benedict had learnt the secrets of the interior life by the roadside, by his own empirical methods, just as he had picked up foreign languages. And now, in April 1782, he told Father Almerici that he could no longer keep his meditations distinct from one another. How could he separate the Power of God and the abasement willed by the Word, the Father creating the stars and the Son bound prisoner by the soldiers under the olive trees of Gethsemane? "When I set about thinking of the Crowning with Thorns, I feel myself drawn up to the Trinity". The monk listened to this strange statement. He realised that the haggard beggar had reached the height of the mystical life, that the cycle of his trials and initiations would soon be complete. "What can you, an ignorant man, know of the Trinity?" asked Father Almerici. "I do not know anything", answered Benedict, "but I am carried out of myself".[1]

Benedict Labre only stayed a short time at Loreto. When he mentioned leaving, Gaudentio and Barbara tried to restrain him. "You don't understand", he murmured. "I must go. . . ." What was his secret reason? Benedict seemed to his hosts more recollected, more free from earth than ever before. There was something of the inevitable in his words and his gestures. "We shall meet again next year", hoped the innkeeper. He knew by heart Benedict's "What's the use of writing? We shall meet again, God willing". But the pilgrim did not repeat the usual formula. He announced instead, "I have got to return to my home". When his friends insisted that he tell them what part of France he came from, Benedict finally said "Flanders". As he was leaving, the Soris looked round their shop for something to please him. One year he had agreed to take a rosary, another year a stick to walk with. This time he indicated his crucifix, which was broken, and they gave him a new one.

Gaudentio Sori went some way up the hill, Monreale,

[1] From Father Almerici's evidence in the Beatification Process.

with the pilgrim. He reiterated the usual leavetaking: "We'll meet again next year". Benedict again said that he must return home. But after all, he had made pilgrimages from Germany to Spain—he always ended up on his knees in the Santa Casa. And the good soul repeated quite confidently, "Never mind, we'll meet again". They had reached the top of the hill. Gaily coloured sails glided on the sea below; towards Ancona one could see Mount Conaro where the Camaldolese were praying. Benedict shook his head firmly. "Goodbye, Master. *Addio, Signor Padrone*". And he pointed to the sky. The innkeeper attributed the good turn his temporal affairs had taken to his poor friend, as well as that peace of heart, that abandonment to God he now felt. In the Gospel the disciples at Emmaus besought a stranger not to leave them: "Stay with us. . . ." Gaudentio Sori would have re-echoed their prayer. But the beggar went on his way over the mountains where spring had conquered.

At the beginning of June, the Pope's train returned through by way of Ancona. Pius VI had won only the slightest concessions from Joseph II in Vienna. Even he had not managed to defend the rights of the contemplative orders, and the life of prayer alone.

But with him Pius VI brought vestments and jewels, the Emperor's official gifts.

Chapter Eight

Vox Populi

ON Good Friday 1783, Benedict was in St. Ignatius'
Church, where the Jesuits—now dissolved—had been replaced by Capuchins. Illness prevented him that Easter
from leaving Rome to go to Loreto. Father Marconi, his
confessor, saw him near the Lady Altar between two
pillars, leaning on his stick, looking more emaciated and
unkempt than ever. If he had not looked so happy, he
would have been terrifying. It was not the first time that
Father Marconi had observed a strange radiance about
him. "One had only to see him", he wrote, "even in the
rags he wore towards the end, to feel an unaccountable
stirring of absolute joy". The poor man talked to Father
Marconi, and as he listened, he looked at the arms emerg-
ing from the sleeves, the arms of a skeleton, with just
enough flesh to nourish the vermin that never left them
alone. Benedict told his confessor that he was now free
of all temptation. Father Marconi knew what that peace
meant: it was the prelude to death. "Youth is full of
wickedness", explained Benedict when people criticised
his mortifications; "it must be subdued".

Vox Populi

Gioventu fiorita e bella. . . . sang the voices at harvest-time, to the strumming of guitars. "Youth is full of wickedness. . . ." The man who spoke thus owed all his greatness to his youth. If he had grown to maturity, his asceticism would probably have been modified, and would surely have struck us less forcibly. At twenty-one one longs for the absolute, and Benedict attained the absolute with his rags. His holiness was one of those passions of youth, going all out for what they want, consuming body and soul. His adolescent logic had always demanded the most perfect, the most difficult way of life; he had become a creature whom housekeepers would have swept out with the garbage he fed on, with the mange-ridden dogs that fed with him. And yet, a former Jesuit named Fraja suddenly knelt down one day before Benedict, and when the beggar trembled with shame at this, the priest told him he was venerating Christ in the person of His poor.

"He is going to die", thought Father Marconi, as his penitent left him. "He is going to die of asceticism and charity". Free from temptation! *Et ne nos inducas in tentationem.* His daily prayer had been heard. That inseparable companion Brother Ass had ceased to be Brother Enemy. But Benedict had been created for struggle, and the time when tranquillity came could only be the time for death.

On Palm Sunday, on the deserted space between St. John Lateran and the Santa Croce, as the sunshine lit up the Sabine Hills, a poor man was slowly walking along by himself, so weak that he looked like falling with every step. A woman gazed after him, murmuring, "Poor Benedict!" Her name was Dominica Bravi, and she knew well the man she was pitying. When he used to lie under the trees in the Colosseum she would bring him oranges and fresh eggs. He would seldom take them, and then only in order not to disappoint her. He assured her that bread dipped in the water of the fountains was quite good enough for such people as he, that he was a sinner and must learn to suffer: *Bisogna saper soffrire*. When he did take an orange, he ate it skin and all without peeling it; with his serene smile, he assured her, "It is good for the stomach". Dominica Bravi had one day said to Benedict, "How wonderful it is to know God by faith and love Him by charity!" And this had overwhelmed him with delight. But she remembered particularly one meeting with him during a time of great gravity and stress. The immense bell of the Capitol had rung out the death of Pope Clement XIV. A litter drawn by white mules, followed by members of penitential sodalities bearing candles, reciting the penitential psalms, had borne from the Quirinale to the Vatican a body putrefying so rapidly that the word "poison" was whispered. This Roman woman remembered as if it had been yesterday the tolling of bells and the sinister rumour. The conclave had opened to elect a successor. Difficult, endless, it had dragged on for four months; as usual, a net of intrigue surrounded the Cardinals, shut up in the Vatican; lampoons were circulating. And while a curious and frivolous Rome wild with the excitement of the competition for the papacy lost itself in speculations, Benedict Labre journeyed from church to church and Dominica Bravi encountered him near St. Paul's-without-the-Walls. "Benedict", she said, "it is a serious moment when a Pope is being chosen. We must pray for Christ's Church". At these words, "Christ's Church", he became transfigured. Sad, motionless, like a beggar carved in stone, he was touching the heights of prayer. And Dominica Bravi came then to understand—in the fashion of the simple and unlearned—that there was an essential and indestructible link between this foreigner whose very surname was unknown to her and the august personages deliberating at the Vatican. The Church, Christ's Church, depended on this anchorite because of the spirit within him which had the power to renew the rites, to strengthen a failing body. More than eight years had gone by since that meeting, and since the cannon of San Angelo had saluted Pius VI's election. Benedict was still the sorrowful pilgrim, and on this Palm Sunday he was making his way to the Santa Croce, where the relics of the Passion were kept. Dominica Bravi realised that she had seen the last of the pilgrim of the Colosseum.

On Monday in Holy week a secular priest called Balducci was preparing to say Mass in San Ignacio. He knelt on the altar steps and said: *"Introibo ad Altare Dei, ad Deum qui laetificat iuventutem meam. . . ."* The words he usually slipped out so mechanically stood out today from his soul in all their full meaning of youth, dawn, purity. The priest was seized by an intense desire to be set free not only from sin but from his own dark shadow. Whence came the wind that carried these liturgical formulae heavenwards? Whence came this longing for a new birth? "I had never said Mass so fervently", said Balducci afterwards. He turned towards his little congregation: a few women with kerchiefs on their heads, and in a corner, some way off because of the disgust he inspired, an indefinable being, a heap of rags whence emerged the face of Christ. Benedict Labre the beggar was very ill, coughing until you thought his chest would burst. The priest looked towards the tattered creature and felt certain that there was the fire whose light was dazzling his soul. He was sure this poor man could see into people's hearts; he felt him gazing into his own. As he progressed in renewing the Sacrifice of the Cross at the altar, the invocations for forgiveness rose more and more earnestly, adoringly, to his lips: *Agnus Dei qui tollis peccata mundi.* . . . "I prayed that God would purify my soul more and more", Balducci was later to say, "that I might become worthy to give Communion to this poor man whom I felt to be a saint". Benedict came to the rail and the priest, who had received an invisible Communion from the poor man, now gave him the Host. One of the most flagrant abuses in the Church at that time was rushing through the offices. Alphonsus Liguori, who used to write and distribute pamphlets calling for a reform of the clergy, denounced with horror their hurrying through Mass (*la messa strappazzata*).

Benedict had also received Communion the previous Friday, the day he told Father Marconi that he was free of temptation. And not only of temptations, but of scruples, of every last bit of attachment to himself and his sorrow. Benedict abandoned that miserable sense of unworthiness he had been too much attached to; he tore off the last clinging shred of the old man. Having offered everything to God, and detached himself even from his detachment, he entered into that fulness of joy which can only come when the soul has stripped itself of everything. He turned a smiling face towards the Host.

That same Monday Benedict's presence is also recorded at the Church of the Holy Apostles. On Tuesday he was

seen in Saint Praxedes, in front of the Column of the
Flagellation. Saint Praxedes' Church was very near Mancini's hostel; and yet Louis Rossi, prefect of the Maronite
college, met Benedict so worn out from that short journey
that he could scarcely answer a friendly greeting. The
cleric passed, followed by his students, young orientals
who gazed with their dark eyes at the ascetic. Benedict
had said a few days before to the old Persian Zitli: "Pray
for me: we shall not meet again".

Wednesday in Holy Week—April 16—when Benedict
wanted to go to Mass, the warden of the hospice tried to
prevent him—he could scarcely stand. Benedict simply
asked for a stronger stick to replace the one that was
bending as he rested his weight heavily on it. He per-
suaded the warden to let him go out just as usual. "You
obstinate fool, you'll die in the street", cried the poor
fellow. "What matter!" sighed Benedict. He dragged
himself along to the Madonna dei Monti.

The service for Wednesday in Holy Week at the
Madonna dei Monti that year would never be forgotten.
The usual congregation: innkeepers, carters, washer-
women, small market-gardeners. They knew Benedict
well; they called him by his Christian name except when
a strange reticence forbade this familiarity. "I felt such
respect for him", recorded one of these simple Romans,
"that I didn't want to call him Benedict, but *Il Signor
Benedetto*"[1]. The whisper went round that he was another Saint Alexis. Did he not work miracles just like a
saint? A groom of the Casa Colonna and a little student
from Santa Maria dei Monti both attributed cures to him.
The student had scrofula, and following Benedict's advice,

[1] Witness given by Cremaschi.

rubbed his throat with oil from the lamp burning in front of Our Lady, whereupon the trouble vanished. When called to witness in the Beatification Process the people from this district produced a great many memories of *Il Signor Benedetto,* varying tremendously in value. "I once noticed him wearing a clean smooth shirt which I suppose was given him in charity", said one. Another stated with the same matter-of-fact air that Benedict had bilocated; that one Christmas night he had been seen praying in the Madonna dei Monti, while he was sleeping among the other poor men behind the bolted doors of the Evangelical Hospice. But this wonderworker was first and foremost a man of prayer. These simple folk, the witnesses of his sanctity, knew that for Benedict the liturgy was the essential rhythm of life. When the Octave of Christmas came round, Benedict would go up to the Ara Coeli to hear the children give their sermons in front of the famous statue of the Bambino, and the pilgrim's face would light up. To celebrate the Resurrection, this man who never ate meat would have a little paschal lamb. On Good Friday it was noticed that he drank vinegar, in memory of Christ given gall to drink. The sorrowful feasts meant more to him than the mysteries of divine joy. In December, when the shepherds who had come down from the Abbruzzi were playing their pipes at every crossroads, Benedict was venerating the famous crib at Saint Mary Major, but in all seasons he would climb on his knees the *Scala Santa,* in memory of the staircase Christ climbed on the eve of his death. Suffering, it was always suffering. It was because they realised this that the faithful now gathered in the Madonna dei Monti were stirred when the priest began to read the Passion. They

were alive to two dramas—Christ's and Benedict's. And
the two mingled together; without that story now being
told slowly over at the altar, the story of Benedict had
no meaning. He was near death, and the Passion would
probably hasten matters. Gardeners, artisans, one said to
another: "Benedict will die at the same time as Christ.
He will fall at the *Exspiravit*".

By a tremendous effort, Benedict rose to his feet. Standing, he listened in complete and total calm to the story
which usually quite overwhelmed him. The smile from
his last Communion seemed not to have left his lips, on
which a silent *Alleluia* seemed to quiver. Christ dragged
from one tribunal to another, the carrying of the Cross
up to Calvary, the noise of hammer on nail: all mingled
together in contemplation of the immovable Godhead.
Benedict Labre could have said with the mystic Angela
de Foligno, reaching the same heights: "The Passion is
for me only a light leading me". *Exspiravit,* pronounced
the priest. The anxious congregation did not see Benedict
waver. But later, on his way out of the church, he collapsed on the steps: a poor wretch fainting from hunger,
a mishap of no importance. Neighbours brought him a
cordial. Zaccarelli the butcher came by. Benedict opened
his eyes again, feebly. "My poor Benedict. . . . how ill you
look. . . . very ill. *Benedetto mio, quanto sta male, molto
male.* Poor Benedict!" The butcher poured out his heart
in compassion. "Come to my house, Benedict, will you?"
The pale lips stirred. Zaccarelli caught the words of acceptance: "Your house. . . . I would love to". How often
had the butcher besought Benedict in vain to come to
his house! He had asked him to have his meals behind
the shop, out of the wind and the sun. But Benedict an-

swered, "Why should I? I eat in the street", and went on his way with his handful of chestnuts. Zaccarelli had told Benedict that he wanted to give him a coat, but he must come and try it for size. Benedict said simply. "Keep it for some poor man who is more in need of it". Zaccarelli invented all sorts of reasons: "I wanted my house to be honoured by his presence", he admitted afterwards. Notions of temporal and spiritual profit were mingled inextricably in his charity. And now, here was Benedict, "the French saint", consenting to come into his house to die! Some of the crowd were at once envious. A practical and prudent priest said to Zaccarelli: "Why take on this burden?" So many hospices would have provided for the beggar. But Zaccarelli was thinking not of the difficult work of mercy he was performing, but of the grace he would be receiving. The priest did not quite understand.

The butcher called his son, Giovanni Paolo, to support Benedict. An apothecary's apprentice happened to be on the spot and also helped. Zaccarelli lived in the Via dei Serpenti, quite close to the Madonna dei Monti. In his semi-conscious state Benedict, still a Trappist in spirit, remembered that the Trappists always lay on straw and ashes to die. "The ground", he managed to say. "Just put me on the ground". His benefactors did not understand what he wanted; they laid down their burden on the first rough bed they came to. "You are tired, Benedict; you want to go to sleep", said the butcher. "Yes, I am tired, I want to sleep". Those were the last clear words he said. He took with him his treasure of silence, his secret. All remedies proved useless: the thin soup forced through the clenched teeth by the good Zaccarelli, a Savoy cake soaked in wine, mustard plasters put to the soles of his feet. Father Piccilli, a member of the Congregazione delle Opere Pie, came as fast as he could to the butcher's house. He held Benedict in the highest esteem; he described how, whenever he got into the pulpit and saw the young beggar in his congregation, he spoke of Our Lord with extraordinary fire, and in words that surprised even himself. But alas! it was to be feared that this Frenchman was more or less tainted with the heresy of his country, Jansenism. Among all the churches of the neighbourhood grouped so close together, Santa Maria dei Monti, San Salvatore dei Monti, San Martino dei Monti, San Francisco de Paula, who ever saw him receive Communion? Father Piccilli rushed along to convert Benedict if he had in truth been heretical. He exhorted the motionless figure, he preached to the man who inspired such eloquence. "Benedict, think of your soul . . . think of eternity". Benedict, who had never thought of anything else, was silent. His only movement had been to cross his arms on his chest in the attitude in which he always prayed—it was instinctive with him. He was roused only for a moment, when Father Piccilli tried to find out whether he had been to Communion lately. "A little . . . Poco . . . poco", words faltered out by a man whose life was hanging on a thread; the priest's doubts remained. Benedict had in fact been to Communion two days before: but he died under a cloud only slowly to disperse. The curate of San Salvatore dei Monti gave him Extreme Unction, but said that he was too ill to receive the Viaticum.

The faint, continued moaning of Benedict mingled with the prayers recited by the Padri della Penitenza, whose work was to assist the dying. And then a bell sounded, and then another, and then all the bells of Rome, in that lovely deep booming that was the prelude to the lenten night when no palace was flood-lit, and the merry music of the harpsichords was muffled. Pius VI, while he allowed a mitigation of the fast, ordered that at nightfall the Salve Regina should be recited while the bells were rung, for the intentions of the suffering Church. All the faithful were invoking Our Lady: *Ad te suspiramus, gementes et flentes.* . . . It was the hymn the schoolchildren sang at the end of class in Amettes in Artois. *Ora pro nobis.* The Padri della Penitenza bent towards the beggar Benedict Joseph Labre and added: *Ora pro eo.* As the bells rang out, there ended a life which would always be held in derision because humanly speaking it could never be proved other than useless.

In Loreto that evening, Gaudentio and Barbara Sori were expecting the pilgrim to arrive. Wasn't this the time he always came? But their little boy Guiseppe, just like children who can say the most terrifying things while playing happily on, because they do not really understand them, said: "Benedict is dying. . . . He is dead", the child insisted. This time Guiseppe was scolded for saying such things. But he suddenly assumed a gravity far beyond his years and added: "Benedict has gone to heaven, I know it in my heart". Guiseppe and Barbara scolded him no more, but sat reflecting and weeping. It was just nightfall.

Maundy Thursday dawned in Rome. The streets were crammed with children. They flowed out of every hovel, every cellar, like swarms of alley-cats. And they shouted: "The saint is dead, *E morto il santo*". Urchins were transformed into heralds of sanctity who had, more than likely, been insulting the beggar, their favourite butt, the day before in the Piazza di Trajano: "*Gabbamondo* . . . Hypocrite . . . Lazy ne'er-do-well . . . *Santocchio*". What trickery could not get a hearing among these naive people! Benedict Labre could quite easily have been a mere impostor. The tragic beauty of his history was that he was not. The fishwives were telling passers-by of the saint's death. What saint? Why, "Our Lady's pilgrim", "the beggar of the Forty Hours", "the penitent of the Colosseum", "the second Saint Alexis", "Benedict the holy Frenchman!"

In the Via dei Serpenti the ovation grew louder and louder: *Beato lui! Beato!* Zaccarelli emptied out the beggar's wallet and listed its contents: *Beato lui!* The clamour grew menacing. Devotees broke into the death room, a relic-hunting crew whom Zaccarelli did not trust a yard. He carefully put the pilgrim's books in order: a much-worn Breviary, a Latin *Imitation of Christ;* the *Memorial of the Christian Life,* by Luis of Granada, the Dominican; the spiritual treatise, by Lansperg entitled *Epistle of Jesus Christ to faithful souls;* a few pious pamphlets: devotions for the Stations of the Cross, the Office of the Seven Dolours of Our Lady. And then some pictures: the Bambino of the Ara Coeli, Our Lady of Loreto, Christ carrying His cross; there were also some significant prayers copied out by hand: a prayer in which the Christian offers the blood of Christ to God the Father, acts of Faith, Hope and Charity, copied out four times by Benedict himself on some day of spiritual desolation. There were also a few silver and copper coins, a torn calendar, some orange and lemon peelings and a few hard crusts. The luggage of a mystic and a vagrant. Zaccarelli also took from the wallet a bundle of papers which priests were later to examine with great care: passports, certificates and such.

The crowd did not confine their acclamations to Benedict, but included in them the whole Zaccarelli family: "How wonderful to have a saint! What luck to have such a treasure!" The lucky ones were meanwhile busy cleaning and washing Benedict's remains. The Congregation of Our Lady of the Snows dressed his body in the usual white garments, and his face, clean at last, was peaceful in its repose. It is said that some nuns—the Maestre Pie who came round from Santa Agatha dei Goti—upon kneeling down by the bed on which he was laid could not bring themselves to recite the De Profundis: instead they intoned the Gloria Patri.

Towards evening, the Brothers of Our Lady of the Snows carried the wasted body over to the Madonna dei Monti. The whole neighbourhood went mad with excitement. *Il santo . . . Ecco il santo. . . .* They cheered and clapped as if in a theatre. This sort of popular canonisation was quite a common occurrence in the days when Rome was the papal capital. Eight years before, Paul of the Cross had died, and at once the same bands of children were thronging the streets of Rome with the same cry: *E morto il santo!* The same crowd gathered, armed with rosaries and medals. Then, however, it was a famous missionary, whom two popes—Clement XIV and Pius VI —had visited when illness had prevented his leaving his monastery on the Coelian Hill. But why were such rumours building up round a beggar? "Your cell is your heart, your soul, the temple of the Holy Ghost", Paul of the Cross had taught his Passionists. The whole Monti neighbourhood was paying homage to a poor man's interior life. But unknowingly so. The crowd did not see as far as that—all they wanted was another patron saint.

Zaccarelli managed, not without some difficulty, to get the poor man buried in the Madonna dei Monti, his favourite church. For the chapel of the Neophytes' College and two parishes—San Salvatore dei Monti and San Martino dei Monti—claimed a right to his corpse: the house where he died belonged to one, and the Mancini hospice to the other. But the devotees of the Madonna and of the holy Frenchman Benedict managed to get their way. They were a quarrelsome people. Sometimes, in the course of an argument, the knife meant for cutting onions became the weapon of a murder. At times too, there would be fights in the Forum between the people of the Monti and their fiercer neighbours who crossed the river to challenge them, and fragments of fallen columns served as ammunition. The possession of a saint's body was a splendid excuse for a fight. Four years later, in the kingdom of Naples, two localities were to dispute over the body of Alphonsus Liguori. And on this Maundy Thursday, 1783, round the Madonna dei Monti, shopkeepers who looked rather like pantomime brigands stood prepared to prevent any attempt to carry off their patron, Benedict the beggar. They hid their arms in the folds of their belts, and were prepared, if need arose, to shed blood. But the funeral procession entered the church unmolested, and the formidable-looking characters were exultant in victory: *Il santo . . . Ecco il santo!* The posthumous history of Benedict Labre began—the only part of his story to have any repercussions in history. The religious exuberance of Italy which the young Frenchman had never really understood—which had, in fact, caused much of his suffering—exceeded all bounds over him.

What chance produced such a tumult over that very obscure life and death? There had been nothing like it, we are told, since the death of St. Philip Neri.[1] The whole town rose to honour Benedict Labre—it was a sort of "spiritual earthquake", we are told by those who witnessed it. From the evening of Maundy Thursday until Easter Sunday, he was laid out in the Madonna dei Monti, his body handled, kissed, and pulled apart by unrestrained devotion. The Corsican soldiers standing guard at the gates of Rome were recalled to their barracks nearby to try and keep order; they had to use arms to beat back the crowds. *Beato lui! . . . Beato lui!* And soon there were other cries to be heard: *Grazia! Grazia!* Several dishevelled creatures, with the help of some murderous-looking men, were pushing forward a sick woman on a stretcher.

Foreigners gazed at these scenes from cafés where they sat, Protestant, Anglo-Saxon, the civilised observing these savages. One, a Puritan minister, John Thayer, spoke so mockingly of the beggar Benedict Labre as to have been judged by his friends to have exceeded the bounds of good taste. He came from Boston, and was visiting Europe "in order", he said, "to gain more respect at home". He studied the languages, the customs and the laws; an Englishman, Arthur Young, was travelling at the same time

[1] *Quanto al corpo, immediatamente Dio gli fe prestare onori tali quali mai non si son veduti in Roma da San Filippo Neri in quà* (Vita del venerabile servo di Dio B. G. Labre, da postulatore R. P. D. Gaetano Palma).

Vox Populi

with just that same patient interest. John Thayer studied Catholicism "just as I should have wished", he explained, "to understand the religion of Mohamed if I had been in Constantinople". He admitted that it was not so bad as he had imagined. He took the greatest care, as far as Catholics were concerned, "to believe nothing of them that they did not say themselves", and to this end consulted various priests. Some had disgusted him by their uncomprehendingness, others had attracted him by their knowledge. And he was not preparing to leave Rome without providing himself with some theological works to read in peace when he got home. And then, one April day, he had followed the crowd as a deeply thoughtful hanger-on, and his newly awakened sympathies suddenly collapsed. Hatred won back all its lost ground—how he loathed this rabble clamouring for new saints and stately ceremonies, so like the Romans of old with their bread and circuses! All his irritation revived, the American listened to conversations of which every word seemed specially chosen to disgust him. They told of soup thrown away and rescued by the beggar from manure heaps, and the vermin—even Italian could not make them sound attractive by calling them *gli animaletti*—he used to push back into his sleeves when they were so ungrateful as to escape. The spiritual significance of such a life was lost among these unpleasant anecdotes seen out of their context: they did far more to twist the true story than any legends could. "As a penance", added the good souls who described these things, "as a penance". The American quite naturally felt rather sick. But he could not tear himself away from the fascination of the spectacle.

Saint Benedict Joseph Labre

Coaches poured into the narrow streets, for the aristocracy had decided to follow the lead of the proletariat. Out of one stepped a Cardinal, out of another an ambassador. A footman opened one door for a woman who swept up the church steps: "Princess Rospogliosi", said someone. She had often given alms to Benedict and asked him to pray for her. And he, who never could allow prayer, the duty of all Christians towards one another, to appear merely the reward for giving alms, would answer: "For one another . . . *L'uno per l'altero*". Various processions converged upon the Madonna dei Monti of veiled women who slipped quietly through the uproar: the most strictly cloistered nuns had got permission to pay their respects to the holy beggar's dead body.

The Corsican soldiers, who had never before had so much to do, were mopping their foreheads and striking harder and harder to keep the crowd back. In vain had they put several rows of benches between Benedict and the crowd. His beard had been half cut away, and his hair torn out; they had even cut bits of the white stuff he was wrapped in. The man for whom Rome's enthusiasm was bordering on riot still looked like the poor wretch they used to jeer at. The unswerving logic of his life remained intact—his triumph looked more like a humiliation: it was the only sort of triumph he would have wanted. And yet this jostling crowd was pushing its way towards something of infinite grandeur: a face reduced almost to the size of a child's, with a long thin nose, jutting-out cheekbones—the face of a suffering prince. The legend so dear to the hearts of the credulous sprang up yet again. The whisper went round: "A nobleman who disguised himself for a penance . . . *Qualche cavaliere che volesse stare nascoto nel mondo".* That distinction which was simply a reflection of the man's soul was attributed by these people to worldly distinction. It was a face that preached sacrifice: *My kingdom is not of this world* ... *Seek ye first the kingdom of God and his justice.* . . . The pilgrim had been nothing more than a man in search of truth. And John Thayer, the Puritan minister, realised this. He knew that this poor man would not willingly have made himself an object of revulsion without some strong and personal reason which must be respected.

On Easter Sunday they could not sing either Mass or Vespers in the Madonna dei Monti. To the rigourist for whom no office is ever performed reverently enough, the order of worship was greatly upset. All day the crowd gave noisy honour to a body that remained flexible and free from corruption. In the evening Benedict Labre was buried beneath the age-old picture of Our Lady he had so revered, while an almost inconsolable crowd clamoured a last goodbye: *Ecco il santo* . . . *Eccolo! Beato lui!* . . . As the news spread from Rome over Italy, and eventually over the whole Christian world, the uproar round the tomb grew greater and greater. The over-enthusiasm of the faithful produced such serious disorders that one day those who came to pray found the church closed by order of the ecclesiastical government, and the Corsican guards in front of the door equipped for whatever new measures might be needed to quell indiscipline. Perhaps learned and sceptical Churchmen were thinking of Deacon Paris and the little cemetery of St. Médard.[1]

[1] The Jansenist "saint", Deacon François de Paris, whose followers created such a tumult round his tomb with their ecstasies and pretended miracles that they became known as the "convulsionaries of Saint Médard".

Saint Benedict Joseph Labre

Deacon Paris was like Benedict in the rigour of his fasting, in his vocation to be a victim of expiation, his unfulfilled wish to be a Trappist. But there the likeness ended. All the joy that Deacon Paris lacked—the halo essential to the Catholic saint—shone in Benedict most fully towards the end.

The Cemetery of St. Médard stayed closed—the Madonna dei Monti was reopened after four days. The crowd came back chastened. "Buy a picture of the saint", cried the profiteers in the square outside, showing pretty little Benedicts against pale blue backgrounds with a few rags thrown in for the sake of appearances. The hubbub in the Via dei Serpenti went on. People known by all the Colosseum district as incurable had regained their health—Angelica Gardelini, for instance, who had been bedridden for a very long time after falling down a flight of stairs. On May 3, a Roman doctor told his sister —a nun in the Carmel at Cavaillon—that there had been sixty-three incontestable miracles. "The dumb speak", he wrote, "the blind see, and paralysis and dropsy have been cured instantaneously. Only last Sunday a woman with dropsy was cured on the flagstone that covers the tomb . . . And unbelievers have been moved to tears like everyone else . . . No one here has ever seen anything like it . . . Tremendous force is needed to control the crowds".[1] For weeks and weeks the crowds kept coming to the Via dei Serpenti with the same cry, *Miracolo!* One foreigner sought the explanation of it all: the Puritan John Thayer, tight-lipped and disapproving but still staying to watch. That was how he heard that a nun in the

[1] Letter published in Abbé Dinouard's *Journal Ecclesiastique* (October 1783).

convent of St. Apollinaris, Maria Brunne, said to be incurable, had just been cured through Benedict Labre's intercession. He set off for the convent, wondering as he went whether Catholicism were error or truth.

For Cardinal de Bernis it was enough that Catholicism was the religion of France and her king. What was worrying the Ambassador at the moment was certainly no abstract point of doctrine, but a small and disagreeable piece of fact: the populace about the Colosseum had prematurely raised to the altar one of the beggars who had often received soup from his own back door. Had the man been an Italian, Bernis would merely have smiled over it. But Benedict was French. And the priests who ate cinnamon ices in the Cardinal's salons in the evening took mischievous delight in congratulating him on the honour Rome was paying France. Bernis' affability froze visibly at the mention of Benedict Labre the beggar, for the whole thing exuded bad taste, ill-breeding, and, worse, fanaticism. The spiritual life of a beggar! It was not an idea that had come his way before, for he was more of a diplomat than a priest. From the *palazzo* where he gave his famous receptions, he watched to see that no shadow of ridicule ever touched the honour of his country or his king. That was his job, that was his duty. On April 30, Bernis informed the Comte de Vergennes, foreign minister at Versailles, "We have here, in one of the city churches, a sight which has been going on since the 16th of this month, which edifies some and gives scandal to others. . . ." Bernis here gave a brief résumé of the life of the beggar, "Labre or Labré"—for his name had been Italianised—"native of a village in the diocese of Boulogne", and once a novice at Septfonts. Why this popular canonisation? A Jesuit intrigue, declared Cardinal de Bernis. It was they who had dragged him from his obscurity. "As soon as he was dead, rumours of his sanctity were at once flying all over the capital, which would seem to prove that the dominant party here (which is the Jesuit party) has singled out this devout beggar for some advantage they think they will get from it. This pious comedy will probably not end as quickly as it has begun. . . ."[1]

For Bernis, all the ascetical effort made by a young man to free his soul from shackles of the flesh was to be boiled down to that—an intrigue whereby a suppressed congregation evidenced the hidden power it still possessed. At that moment the King of Spain was demanding the canonisation of a seventeenth-century Spanish Bishop named Palafox, well known to be an enemy of the Jesuits. And they, in their turn, were trying to advance this pawn against their defunct opponent on the chessboard of ecclesiastical affairs. They discovered the wretched Benedict, in his rags in the Madonna dei Monti, and thus the whole affair came about. *Combinazione!* Bernis the diplomat was thoughtful. As a noble and a prince of the Church, however, he offered a thousand crowns to support this beatification cause of which he spoke so lightly.

The struggles of conscience that beset John Thayer were reaching their conclusion. That practical man had completed his investigations: he was simply submitting to facts he had himself verified. His fearless logic fitted well with Benedict's holiness. This educated traveller

[1] Archives of Foreign Affairs: *Rome, Correspondance Politique*, Vol. 893.

was getting through to the nourishing substance of the lesson taught by a pilgrim who pretended to nothing but ignorance. Losing one's life to find it. . . . Dying to be reborn. . . . A great spiritual break was imposing itself on the Puritan from Boston because a poor man had acted consistently as his faith led him to. John Thayer was later to write of his uncertainties and struggles and to say that, although the truth was all around him, it had no chance against the prejudices which he had imbibed with his mother's milk. And then, he was a minister: he would have had to give up his station in life and his income; he was affectionate and devoted to his family: he would have had to incur their anger; to put it briefly, his mind was convinced, but his heart was unchanged. He longed to see the light, but was afraid of seeing it too clearly. Yet he tells us that in the end his eternal salvation came uppermost, and he cast himself on his knees.

On May 25, 1783, Rome learnt of the recantation of a well-known foreign visitor, John Thayer, the Puritan minister, one of the first converts in the New World. Soon after, he set sail for home with apostolic work in view.[1]

"There can be no doubt", Cardinal de Bernis informed the Comte de Vergennes on June 4, "that the Jesuit party in Rome are behind the outcry produced by the innumerable miracles attributed to Benedict Joseph Labre of the diocese of Boulogne-sur-Mer. . . ." He spoke of the perpetual stream of the sick and crippled and the con-

---

[1] John Thayer, who attributed his conversion to Benedict Labre, became a Catholic missionary priest and worked for the spread of his faith in the Anglo-Saxon countries. He died in Ireland, in Limerick, in 1816. (See The Catholic Encyclopedia: *Thayer*.)

tinued presence of the Corsican Guard—they were not discharged till the end of June. The Church kept order round the tomb. By July the number of miracles registered had reached a hundred and thirty-six.

Were Roman throats weary from constant cries of *Il Santo! Beato Lui?* As the summer wore on, did the crowds in the Madonna dei Monti get less dense? One witness, Abbé de Lunel, stated in a letter dated July 6 in Rome that the little church, "full from morning till night" had become "better known than St. Peter's".[1] But Bernis spoke quite differently. From his Alban villa he told Vergennes of a great decrease in fervour and gave the reason: it had emerged that Benedict Labre not only himself read the sermons of Père Le Jeune—"an intimate friend of the famous Père Quesnel"—but, still worse, made his parents read them too:

This suspicion of Jansenism (wrote Bernis on July 29) has begun to make the enthusiasm of the Jesuit party who were promoting and admiring the sanctity and the supposed miracles of this French beggar cool off considerably; each day the visitors to his tomb grow fewer. They will no doubt allow this small remains of fanaticism to die a natural death that they may not have to admit how grossly they were mistaken. . . . It now appears that when this beggar was dying he was offered the sacraments, and replied that that was not necessary. His parish priest continues to assert that whatever else may be thought of him, he would never make his Easter duties in his parish church. . . .

. . . This whole affair will probably end, as I foresaw,

[1] *Miscellany of later miracles . . . and other documents, letters, extracts from letters* etc. (1784).

in utter farce, and all that is needed to complete it is for the Jansenist party to acclaim the miracles of one of their proselytes when the Jesuits have finally abandoned him. Nothing is impossible where fanaticism is concerned; but it makes religion suffer and look ridiculous in the eyes of heretics and unbelievers. . . .[1]

Friends of the Jesuits and the Jansenists were fighting to patronise Benedict Labre! In September, noted Cardinal de Bernis, the Jesuits were in the lead, and he wondered what doubtful end they had in view. The beggar became a plaything of the different cliques, as a sort of completion to his great humiliation. For his whole life had been a burning effort to grasp the essential element in religion and purify it from alloy at a time when it was so firmly in the grasp of worldly interests as to be almost suffocated. He was like the true poet freeing his art from all that is foreign to it, from all the dead weight that would hamper his song in its ascent.

Could the order of charity, the order of sanctity whose preëminence Pascal proclaimed, still be salvaged?

In their house at Amettes, Jean Baptiste Labre and Anne Barbe Gransire were getting old. They had heard nothing of Benedict since a young Artesian, returning from Rome, had brought them the message from his old friend whom he met at St. Louis-des-Français: "Present my compliments; tell them I'm happy". When beggars came past along the road, Anne Barbe gave them alms with gentler charity than of old. But now the departed

[1] *Archives of Foreign Affairs:* "Rome, Correspondance Politique", Vol. 894.

was coming back to the orchards of his childhood, like a man raised from the dead, calling everyone by their familiar names but cut off from them by the radiance shining round him. His Beatification cause had been introduced the day after he died. In June 1783, Playoult, the parish priest of Amettes, and Bourgeois, his curate, opened the preliminary investigations. The following year Mgr. de Partz de Pressy summoned Jean Baptiste Labre and Anne Barbe Gransire to come and give evidence before him about their son. They stayed in his palace and dined at his table. All Boulogne was moved by seeing the aged Bishop, so loved by his people, between these two peasants; and as was the fashion then, the group was made the subject of engravings. Benedict's parents answered the questions put to them in the undemonstrative fashion of villagers more given to placidity than astonishment. But when they learnt of the suspicion of Jansenism which threatened to tarnish Benedict's memory in Italy they fired up and protested, for they loathed Jansenism utterly, though they would have been hard put to it to define what it was. Abbé Jacques Joseph Vincent, the former curate of Conteville, defended his nephew warmly and declared himself willing to go to the stake for the purity of his faith and the steadfastness of his hope.

While Benedict's followers in Italy were hearing the name of Amettes in Artois, Anne Barbe Gransire came to hear how the Soris, shopkeepers in Loreto, had taken in her son when he was exhausted and shivering with cold. By means of a pilgrim who "went to wait upon" the Holy House, Benedict Labre's mother got into touch with the hostess who had taken such compassion on him. On

Vox Populi

January 20, 1785, gratitude inspired the woman from Artois to write the following letter:

Madame,

The kind letter and holy cards which you sent me by the pilgrim, François Jacques Amand Alender, gave me real pleasure. The young man seemed delighted with his journey and expressed the greatest gratitude for your kindness to him during his stay in Loreto; he begs me to tell you in this letter that he will remember it all his life. My husband, my family and I are in the same state; we will never forget the extraordinary goodness you showed to our dear son, now dead, Benedict Joseph, on his pilgrimages to Loreto. You tell me what a consolation it must be to me to have given birth to such a child, and I acknowledge, Madame, that it is, but is it anything to be proud of? I humbly recognise that a father and mother are only the worthless instruments used by God to give bodily life to their children. Therefore if Benedict Joseph, our very dear son, became holy on this earth by the practice of humility and the other Christian virtues, I must freely admit that his behaviour, or rather the life of virtue which he led even from childhood, was purely the effect of God's grace and therefore the work of the Holy Ghost alone: and I thank God for it every day and beg Him most earnestly to grant to you most abundantly the same help so that you may come to the same one day. I also pray this for your dear kind family whom I wish I could embrace with all my heart. At the moment, Madame, that is the only way I can show my gratitude. My joy would be complete if I could fly to you and accept your generous invitation, but as I cannot now undertake such a long and difficult journey, will you allow me at least to assure you of my deepest respect, and also that of my husband and my little family, and tell you that we

209

will all continue to pray for the temporal and spiritual prosperity of your own dear family.

In these sentiments, Madame, I have the honour to be, most affectionately, your humble and obedient servant,

Anne Barbe Gransire.

Amettes, January 20, 1785.[1]

The letter was addressed to *Madame Barbe Soury* (*Sori*), Innkeeper at the Sign of Benedict Joseph Labre. Eighteen months after his death, his name was being used as an advertisement: the innkeeper in Loreto was boasting because he had been her guest, while the peasant in Amettes did not want to be honoured because he was her son!

And very soon the "great fire" which Benedict had seen ravaging his country in prophetic dreams broke out. While the Reign of Terror was ruling France, the investigations which were to end in the canonisation of the pilgrim were going quietly on in the Church's own good time.[2] One priest called as a witness in this peaceful affair stated, in the tragic year of 1793, "that there was no place in either France or Italy that Benedict Labre's fame had not reached".

A devotion not yet authorised by the Church was spreading in France during the period when clandestine Masses were said in barns transformed into chapels. Persecuted Catholics took Benedict for their patron. And the name of this man—so merciful that he would not

[1] The original letter may be seen in Rome in the convent of the Sisters of Mary Immaculate, together with the letter written by Benedict to his parents after leaving Septfonts.

[2] Benedict Labre was beatified May 20, 1860, and canonised December 8, 1883.

permit himself to curse even the devil—became so suspect under the new régime that in 1794 Le Bon sent two Artesian women to the scaffold simply for being in possession, "among other fanatical objects", of relics of Benedict Joseph Labre.[1] By the light of the "great fire" Benedict's features stood out sharply in their desolation. The monasteries he had tried in vain to enter went up like haystacks. Priests—God's priests whom he had revered—slipped from indifference into apostasy, and talked of the ceremonies which had been his whole life as "juggling" and "play-acting". On roads where the pilgrim had winced to hear a cart-driver abuse the name of God as he goaded on his mules, men were singing loud and impious songs with all the strength of their youth and conviction:

> O Trinity of our ancestors, what are you
> Compared with our trinity of the tricolor?

The Trinity! The Divine Trinity! The dogma Benedict talked of with the Franciscans at Loreto! A whole mystical world seemed to be being abolished, the God-centred ethos of the beggar Benedict Labre. The altar of patriotism was replacing an altar which claimed only one victim, ever unchanging.

The first hymns in honour of Benedict Labre were, despite their poverty of rhyme and mediocrity of style, very touching. Abbé Caron composed several for the French émigrés in London whose apostle he constituted himself. In France women who still secretly said their Hail Marys used to sing to the most elementary tunes:

[1] They were Adrienne Dupont (from Saint Hilaire) and Hyacinthe Lagache (from Vaudricourt). Deramecourt, *Le clergé du diocèse d'Arras, Boulogne et Saint-Omer pendant la Revolution.*

Saint Benedict Joseph Labre

Le courageux Athlète
L'Ami du Roi des rois
Etait natif d'Amettes
Village dans l'Artois.

Was that village imbued with some spirit of strength? After the civil constitution of the clergy had been passed, priests whose consciences were in agony gathered under the joists of the garret where the drama of Benedict's youth was played. And a great many of the refractory clergy made pilgrimages to Amettes on their way to exile.

In the middle of the Revolution, Louis Labre, a brother of Benedict's but one who had scarcely known him, went to be ordained at Ypres. But Jacques Labre, the second son, a priest now for twenty years, lived still in his parents' old house. He wore his cassock, and no one dreamt of persecuting him. Perhaps he had meditated too long on Père l'Aveugle's sermons. The disease of scruples that Benedict had finally conquered had beaten this weaker brother. His nervous distress prevented him from saying Mass. And the poor man was respected by all around him. But during the summer of 1793, a slight uprising started nearby. Trees of liberty were being cut down, tricolor cockades torn off. This disturbance which was as little violent as a disturbance could well be was later known as *La Petite Vendée d'Artois*. One August day, a troop of soldiers from Béthune who had gone to repress it came through Amettes, drunk with wine and easy victory; they were congratulating themselves on having put down the tyrants when suddenly at a crossroads they saw a picture peaceful enough to madden them. A little chapel in honour of Our Lady, and a priest not even pretending to be anything else, walking up and down, book in hand, with apparently no suspicion of the change that had come over the world. It was Abbé Jacques Labre saying his office. The peace Benedict had finally won was gradually returning to him too. His elder brother had led him on too strait a path and was now, no doubt, taking mercy on him from heaven. As dawn broke upon his soul, Abbé Jacques Labre was praying to his brother. He was a man of weakness and humility.

With fury the commandant of the troop stared at this rebel against the law. With one blow from his sword he struck him down. The victim collapsed without a sound, and then stood up again and, with the same politeness with which Benedict Labre used to treat even the worst ruffians, Abbé Jacques Labre bowed to the man who thought he had killed him; he went on saying his office —like an indestructible ghost of the past, a priest invulnerable. It is said that the whole troop of revolutionaries were seized with a superstitious terror and fled from Amettes, the hive of fanaticism they were setting out to destroy.

According to a tradition of the place, that is why Benedict Joseph Labre's house was preserved. There at the foot of its sloping meadows, peasant women pray to the poor man who listened so willingly to the grievances of humble folk, and the mystery of his life does not worry them at all.